INTERIOR
MATERIALS & SURFACES
THE COMPLETE GUIDE

INTERIOR
MATERIALS & SURFACES
THE COMPLETE GUIDE

HELEN BOWERS

FIREFLY BOOKS

A FIREFLY BOOK

Published by Firefly Books Ltd. 2005

First printing

Publisher Cataloging-in-Publication Data (U.S.)
Bowers, Helen.
    Interior materials and surfaces : the complete guide / Helen Bowers—1st ed.
[256] p. : col. photos ; cm.
Includes index.
Summary: A technical, practical and aesthetic guide to the range of materials
available for do-it-yourself projects and home decorating. Covers woods,
metals, plastics, glass, fabrics, papers, leather, paints, ceramics, concrete
and plaster. Advises on conventional and unusual uses for each material,
plus information on sources, cost, specifications, maintenance and safety.
ISBN 1-55297-967-9
ISBN 1-55297-966-0 (pbk.)
1. Decoration and ornament. 2. Artists' materials. 3. Interior decoration. I. Title.
747 22   NK2115.B69 2005

Library and Archives Canada Cataloguing in Publication
Bowers, Helen, 1964-
        Interior materials and surfaces : the complete guide / Helen Bowers.
Includes index.
ISBN 1-55297-967-9 (bound).--ISBN 1-55297-966-0 (pbk.)
        1. Building materials. 2. Interior decoration. I. Title.
TH8025.B69 2005   698   C2004-905040-0

Published in the United States by
Firefly Books (U.S.) Inc.
P.O. Box 1338, Ellicott Station
Buffalo, New York 14205

Published in Canada by
Firefly Books Ltd.
66 Leek Crescent
Richmond Hill, Ontario L4B 1H1

This book was conceived, designed, and produced by
THE IVY PRESS LIMITED
The Old Candlemakers, West Street,
Lewes, East Sussex BN7 2NZ, U.K.

Creative Director – Peter Bridgewater
Publisher – Sophie Collins
Editorial Director – Jason Hook
Design Manager – Simon Goggin
Senior Project Editor – Caroline Earle
Designer – Joanna Clinch
Photographer – Calvey Taylor-Haw

Printed in China

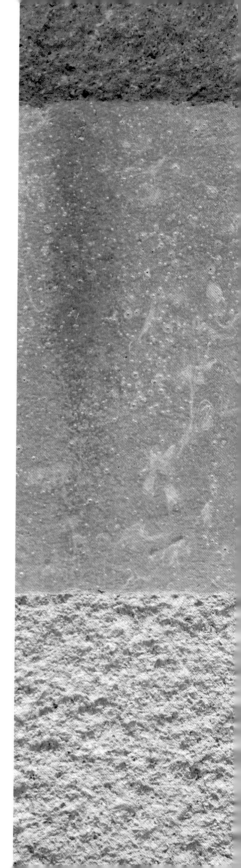

CONTENTS

INTRODUCTION

Interior Materials & Surfaces: The Complete Guide is a practical handbook to use when consulting or instructing an architect, designer or builder, or when working on home projects or home decorating. It aims to inform, so you can choose and discuss materials with confidence, and to inspire you to consider new materials, think about familiar materials in a new way or use traditional or innovative materials in interesting combinations or applications.

The range of materials includes those that have been in use since the beginning of civilization, some that have been developed recently and those that have been popular in the past but which have fallen, perhaps only temporarily, out of fashion. When we decorate our homes or use newly available materials either structurally or decoratively, we are participating in a long tradition of improvement and embellishment. Whether we choose wood, stone or the latest high-tech glass, metal and plastic products, we are perpetuating the tradition of satisfying a basic primal instinct to make a home.

From the time people first constructed tents, tepees or huts, or even just sheltered in caves, they have sought to decorate and furnish their living space to increase the level of comfort, to create a particular atmosphere or to personalize whatever they called home. Since the first use of vegetable pigments and animal fats in cave painting, advances in technology and the access to different materials have been reflected in the development of decorative materials and skills. Almost as soon as a material was developed for communal or industrial purposes, it was refined for use by individuals in their homes. Handworked or industrially manufactured, each material was refined to an increasingly decorative level that transcended its functional requirements. Stonework became beautifully finished and highly textured and stone fittings such as fireplaces and paneling were carved into complicated forms and patterns. Metalwork for brackets, trusses, hinges, tools and household items took on an elegance of form and attention to pattern that had no impact on its mechanical performance.

Since the 1930s, when the first breath of modernism arrived in a domestic context, innovation has vied with tradition in the materials you choose to be at home with, in the interiors you live in every day. Many materials initially used purely for protection from the weather have been superseded by high-performance products, but the original materials still are in demand, for effect even when not used structurally, to provide a visual connection to the tangible tradition of the built environment.

There is now unprecedented choice both in terms of style and the means by which we may achieve it. We may not only select rustic, historical, traditional, modern, post-modern, contemporary, cozy or flamboyant, but also decide whether to achieve the look through materials that have been used throughout history or with the help of the latest technology and recently developed materials and techniques. These decisions must be set against the context of budget and available craftsmanship as well as concerns with modern performance requirements in areas such as sound and heat insulation, durability and, now, a knowledge of the effect using different materials can have on our global environment.

This wealth of possibilities has not made decision-making any easier. All too often we are faced with a material or finish that we like but which we are not sure how to use, or a room that demands a special treatment but we don't quite know what. This book is here to help in these situations. It supplies the answers to questions about the suitability of a finish or material for a particular purpose, and provides the technical information you need to work in successful partnership with a consultant or decorator on an unfamiliar idea.

It also helps you look afresh at familiar materials and broaden your horizons on what is available. Included here are ideas for materials such as leather and paper, which are still manufactured much as they have been for centuries, and innovative suggestions for nontraditional decorating materials such as plastics and woven metals. You may find yourself reconsidering materials that you had dismissed on grounds of cost. Many materials that have always been considered luxury finishes, such as marble and steel, are now, due to highly mechanized processing and computer-aided fabrication, affordable and readily available in small quantities, and in a form that can be used in a domestic setting. The cost guides are numbered from 1 to 5 — very low, low, medium, high and very high. Each rating has been based on approximate cost levels within each category of material.

As well as being a useful guide to the things you know you want, this book is intended to be a sourcebook for finishes and effects you didn't know you could have. Many materials that are commonly used in the building industry are also perfectly appropriate for home use, but have not yet been widely embraced. An increasing number of materials developed specifically for industrial or corporate applications are now available to homeowners, and we can all benefit from the advantages they have brought to the commercial world. Concrete, for example, can be manufactured to very detailed individual specifications by introducing exotic additives, pigments or aggregates for a range of potential unconventional applications. Familiar materials such as glass have been developed to meet very strenuous demands of structural stability with special properties like protection from sunlight. These advanced materials can be manufactured with a wide range of decorative effects and there is every reason to use them to enhance your home.

When stepping into the unfamiliar, it is always useful to find a craftsperson who knows the material intimately to accompany you in developing that material for your specific use. Adventurous use of materials such as steel and glass, which requires detailed calculations and heavy factory conditions for manufacturing components, depends on the use of consultants and fabricators who are experts in the abilities of those materials. There are practitioners in every field ready to push the boundaries to new frontiers who will respond to your vision. There are ideas in this book at all levels, ranging from uses for paper and fabric that you may tackle at home with a pair of scissors and some glue, to projects that may require a whole team of professionals, specialized suppliers and contractors.

This book, however, is only a reference and should not take the place of professional consultation. When making plans to carry out building work, the most effective way to get a great job done is to be able to give clear instructions to your architect, designer or craftspeople, then step back and trust their experience and expertise. The descriptions of materials here should inspire you to go beyond a popular or established application of materials, whether you are using them yourself or to inform you as a client. Either way, you will be armed with a greater knowledge and have the confidence to make decisions about the exciting possibilities that are available and achievable.

WOOD & WOOD COMPOSITES

Wood is so widely present in our daily lives that it often goes unnoticed. In many regions it has always been the primary building material, but it is available in almost every part of the world. It is easily harvested and transported, and can be worked by hand or with basic machine tools.

Harvested wood, known as lumber, is categorized into hardwoods and softwoods, although these are general categories based on density, and in fact some hardwoods are softer than many of the trees classed as softwoods. Hardwoods are the product of deciduous trees, which shed their leaves in the fall and are relatively slow-growing. Softwoods are usually derived from evergreen trees growing in temperate zones, which have sharp, slim needle leaves and seeds that grow in cones. Softwoods also contain a large amount of natural resin and are slightly faster growing than hardwoods. Around 400 species of trees are used in the production of various lumbers. Historically, expanding trade and empire-building has been reflected in the taste for different woods in the home, with local woods falling out of fashion in favor of exotics such as mahogany and rosewood. Awareness of the devastation that clear cutting has caused in tropical forests has affected the demand for exotic lumber, but as the economy of many countries depends on the production of hardwoods, these are increasingly available from managed forests.

Wood is a living material composed of cellulose, which forms the cells and the lignin that binds cells together. As the cells absorb or release atmospheric moisture, they will expand or contract and, consequently, lumber will swell or shrink. This applies even to long-felled lumber, which is why expansion must be accommodated around wood floors and the drying effect of central heating can cause problems in old houses. Different woods are suited to different purposes, depending on the great natural variation in their density, grain and color.

Every home contains wood in some capacity, from external wall and roof coverings to structural lumber, windows, doors, staircases, floors or storage solutions. It has been used as the basic material for furniture-making all over the world, from crude tables and benches to finely turned furniture made with richly grained woods that might also be carved, detailed and inlaid with precious materials. Due to increased mechanization, technological developments and the demands of modern living, new products have arrived on the market as low-cost, easy-to-use, minimal-maintenance alternatives to wood. However, many of these products are not as adaptable as wood to changing styles and ways of living, and people will always enjoy the reassuring warmth and tactile qualities of natural wood surfaces.

SOFTWOOD

Softwoods are obtained from coniferous trees growing naturally in North America and northern Europe. They are available in a number of forms and sizes and are widely used in the construction industry as a building and joinery material, as well as being a popular choice for furniture and surface finishes. Softwoods can be described as a standard, easy-to-use, cost-effective, environmentally friendly raw material.

Properties: The most commonly used softwood trees are spruce, Douglas fir, ponderosa pine, western hemlock and western red cedar. Softwoods will expand and contract with heat and moisture; they can also lighten or darken. They have a lower density than hardwoods, making them good for acoustic and thermal insulation. Being solid but soft, they can be worked by hand or with high-tech machinery. They are flexible and strong, and their strength can be increased by laminating or gluing sections together. Water resistance can be improved by pressure-treating, which leaves a slight greenish tinge. The straight grain and uniform texture are perfect for paint, stain and oil finishes.

Use and Maintenance: Outdoor uses include furniture, landscaping and decking — seal with weatherproof stains, varnish or exterior grade paints. Indoor uses are furniture, flooring and trim. Softwoods can be turned on a lathe to make balustrades or bought as composite blockboards for bookshelves and paneling. The wood should be acclimatized on site for two to three weeks prior to use and sealed with paint, stain, varnish or oil for durability. Treated wood should be cleaned as per the requirements of the sealant. Surfaces can be repaired by sanding back, filling defects and refinishing.

Safety and Environment: Softwoods are a natural, nonpolluting material from a renewable resource. Certified lumber from managed, sustainable forests is stamped to ensure it has been through a tracking system.

Availability: Easily sourced from lumberyards as sawed or planed lumber or profiled moldings such as door frames, crown molding and other trim. Also widely used in prefabricated components such as doors and window frames.

Cost: ❶ Very low.

Specifications: Sawed or planed, in knotty or plain grades, in a wide range of standard and special sizes and lengths.

HARDWOOD

Hardwoods derive from deciduous trees and are available in various forms and sizes. They are used as a building and joinery material, and for surface finishes, furniture and craft ranges, from bowls and kitchen utensils to light fixtures. The great variety of species, and the level of natural variation within each, provide numerous effects, and the rich colors and natural beauty of hardwoods create a feeling of luxury.

Properties: Hardwood trees grow more slowly than conifers (see Softwood, page 13), so their lumber is stronger, denser and homogeneous. Strength varies greatly between species: hickory, the hardest commercially available variety, is five times harder than aspen, a "soft" hardwood. Domestic hardwoods such as oak, ash, maple, beech, cherry and walnut grow in North America and northern Europe. Common exotic hardwoods, from the tropical forests of South America, Africa and Asia, include iroko, mahogany, padouk and teak. Such lumber sourced from original forests is often particularly dense; some varieties are nearly impervious to water. Hardwoods can be hand- or machine-worked. They also expand, contract and change color as they age. Hardwoods resist fire better than softwoods, but charring reduces their strength, so this needs to be allowed for when using structurally.

Use and Maintenance: Use outdoors for furniture and structures, sealing with weatherproof varnish. Indoors, hardwoods are a feature material — use for exposed structural elements, flooring, fixtures such as stair treads and doors and furniture. Hardwoods are available laminated, as veneers (for coverings) or sheets (for shelves). They should be acclimatized on site for two to three weeks before use and sealed with varnish or oil. When cleaning, follow the requirements of the sealant. Repair or refurbish by sanding back and refinishing.

Safety and Environment: Northern hemisphere hardwoods are usually grown in sustainable forests. Some tropical hardwoods are from managed forests, but traffic in this material is intricate and it can be difficult to ensure you are buying from a legitimate producer. Certified lumber is stamped.

Availability: Direct from lumberyards and home-improvement retailers. Reclaimed floors and doors can be sourced from architectural salvage yards.

Cost: ❹ High.

Specifications: Sawed or planed, in knotty or plain grades, in a wide range of standard and special lumber sizes and lengths.

TONGUE AND GROOVE

Tongue and groove (T&G) is a machined lumber board shaped to provide an interlocking system, consisting of a projecting "tongue" along one edge that slots into a corresponding groove on its neighbor. The visible joins often have a clearly arrised (or shaped) edge, usually a V in profile. T&G boards can create a variety of effects, from traditional wall paneling to rustic or sleek modern floorboards.

Properties: T&G wall paneling is usually softwood and often used in conjunction with baseboards and a molding, such as a chair rail, along the top. Boards are held together with pins or clips and fixed onto horizontal softwood furrings (or battens). T&G paneling provides a dependable, even finish, and can conceal deteriorating plaster, slightly increase a wall's acoustic and thermal properties or provide a hardwearing wallcovering. T&G floorboards are usually composite or solid hardwoods and have a minimal or nonexistent arris for a smooth finish.

Use and Maintenance: T&G wall paneling can give a traditional appearance to formal rooms, or a nautical or cottagey feel in bathrooms. Use it to conceal pipework or to make a bathtub panel, but not in areas directly exposed to water. T&G floorboards can be laid on battens or underlay, so are not dependent on the condition of the subfloor (provided it is level). Some types can be laid over underfloor heating, although the wood will absorb a portion of the heat. Softwood boards provide an inexpensive flooring if a certain amount of marking is acceptable. Many floorboards come with a durable factory finish, which will extend the life of the wood. When painting, staining or varnishing boards, remember to cover all six sides prior to installation. Maintenance is dependent on the finish.

Safety and Environment: T&G is environmentally friendly as it is a nontoxic, natural material from a renewable resource. Certified lumber produced from managed and sustainable forests is stamped to ensure it has been through a tracking system.

Availability: T&G softwood board is available from lumberyards or building suppliers. T&G hardwood or composite floorboards are available from flooring companies or home-improvement retailers.

Cost: ❷/❸–❹ T&G softwood board: low. T&G hardwood or composite floorboards: medium to high.

Specifications: T&G softwood board comes in various standard sizes. Hardwood or composite floorboards available in different grades (rustic to plain), in various wood types and usually factory-finished.

PLYWOOD

Plywood is the product of the earliest wood engineering, so can be considered the original lumber sheet material. It is available in a wide range of grades and finishes that are suitable for many different fabrication uses — for manufacturing, construction, home projects and constructing interior surfaces (frameworks) in built-in furniture. This material is efficiently produced, so is a very inexpensive lumber product.

Properties: Ply is manufactured from sheets of cross-laminated wood veneer, which are pressure-bonded under heat with waterproof resin adhesive. Douglas fir, poplar and birch are common veneers. Ply is very strong against impact (and in cross and diagonal tension), lightweight and easy to work with using conventional tools and machines. It is also highly stable when exposed to moisture, usually reverting to its original thickness when dry. It is rated for internal or external use depending on the veneer, glue or treatment. Marine ply or WBP (water- and boil-proof), for instance, is heat- and pressure-treated to improve water resistance. Very thin high grades (flexible plywood) can be curved in one direction.

Use and Maintenance: Traditionally, plywood has been used as a structural, decking or framing material. Today it is also used in exposed situations that emphasize, rather than disguise, its nature. Always choose individual sheets as appearance varies widely. Ply can be sawed, sanded, drilled, nailed, glued and finished, and used for shelving, furniture and paneling. It is effective for kitchen counters: the layers create dramatic edges when sanded and shaped, but all exposed surfaces must be finished with a durable varnish. Ply should be sealed on all sides to prolong life: use paint, stain or varnish (sanding between each coat). It is flammable, so protect if using structurally. Repair damage by sanding back and refinishing.

Safety and Environment: Most sheets of plywood are produced from logs that have been harvested from managed forests and will bear the mark of a certification body. Layers are harvested in parallel along the curve of the log, meaning that the bulk of the lumber is used with little going to waste.

Availability: Widely available from lumberyards and home-improvement retailers.

Cost: ❷ Low.

Specifications: Standard sheets 4 x 8 ft (1,220 x 2,440 mm) in incremental thicknesses, ⅛–1 in (4–25 mm). Some grades up to 4 x 10 ft (1,220 x 3,000 mm), or in thicknesses greater or less than standard.

CHIPBOARD

 Chipboard, or particle board, is a low-cost, basic, rough lumber product made out of wood chips and fashioned into sheets. It is a utilitarian material that is rarely seen as a finishing or facing product itself, but is generally used as a framing or base material in the construction and furniture-making industries. It is also found beneath the laminates or veneers of many ready-formed shelves and work surfaces.

Properties: Chipboard is manufactured from wood chips that are pressure-bonded together under heat using synthetic resin adhesives. Normal-, medium- and high-density grades are produced. Some can be treated to make them flame-retardant or moisture-resistant. All grades (except those specifically treated) are susceptible to moisture, becoming waterlogged before swelling and breaking down. Chipboard is strong in tension and durable against impact. In dry situations it is also very hard-wearing. It is characterized by a rough surface to the sides and edges.

Use and Maintenance: All but the highest grade moisture-resistant chipboard is suitable for indoor use only. This inexpensive material is intended for use as a base for other finishing materials: it is prelaminated in melamine for use as postformed kitchen countertops and is frequently veneered and used for ready-to-assemble furniture. It is also used as carcassing or as a shelving material where a rough finish is desired, or covered in adhesive vinyl for very low-cost shelves and panels. It can be tongued and grooved for use as flooring to underlay a floating wood floor or carpet, or varnished and used as wall paneling for a rudimentary but durable wooden surface. Its rough, absorbent finish makes it unsuitable for fine paintwork, but it is possible to apply a waterproof paint to help protect against moisture.

Safety and Environment: Most chipboard sheets are produced from logs harvested from managed forests with no wastage and will bear the mark of a certification body.

Availability: Widely available at lumberyards and building centers as sheets, precut pieces or shelves veneered in melamine or wood finishes. It is also incorporated in products by suppliers of kitchens and ready-to-assemble furniture.

Cost: ❶ Very low.

Specifications: Standard sheet size 4 x 8 ft (1,220 x 2,440 mm) is generally ⅝ or ⅞ in (18 or 22 mm) thick. Laminated countertops are 2 ft (600 mm) or 3 ft (900 mm) wide, 1½ in (40 mm) thick.

WOOD • RUBBER, PLASTIC, RESIN & LINOLEUM • METAL • GLASS • FABRIC • PAPER • LEATHER • PAINT, VARNISH & LACQUER • STONE, CERAMICS & TILES • CONCRETE & CEMENT • PLASTER

LAMINATED BUTCHER'S BLOCK

INTERIOR MATERIALS & SURFACES: THE COMPLETE GUIDE

LAMINATED BUTCHER'S BLOCK

Laminated butcher's block consists of narrow, uniform strips of hardwood that are glued together with the grain parallel, to form a thick, heavy sheet. The finished blocks are most often used as solid wooden counters or for kitchen backsplashes. They are also used for counters where wider solid planks might warp and mark. Depending on the width of strips used, this can have a chunky or elegant effect.

Properties: Sections of solid hardwood (typically 1½ inches/4 cm wide) are bonded together under pressure with adhesives to form this distinctive wood product. It is available in a wide range of woods, including oak, cherry, maple, beech, walnut and iroko. Its construction makes it extremely dense, durable and unlikely to warp. It is also strongly resistant to abrasion, high temperatures and impact, but can be damaged by repeated exposure to steam. It will resist household stains if treated with an appropriate sealant, but spills should always be wiped up immediately. It is solid and easy to work with hand or machine tools, and is tactile, hard-wearing and luxurious.

Use and Maintenance: Laminated butcher's block can be bought untreated or with a factory-sealed moisture- and steam-resistant surface. Untreated lengths must be primed and sealed on all sides before installing. Even countertops that are to be oil finished must have the underside and ends sealed.

Lengths should be acclimatized on site, but away from wet areas for two weeks. Countertops above dishwashers should have a moisture-proof heat-insulating sheet on the underside for steam protection. Butcher's block also makes attractive tabletops, backsplashes and shelving. Damage should be repaired by sanding back, filling and refinishing. Oiling gives a natural look, but must be reapplied yearly; varnish for durability.

Safety and Environment: Most sheets of laminated butcher's block are produced from logs that have been harvested from managed forests and, being made using small sections of lumber, are nonwasteful.

Availability: Can be sourced from lumberyards, home-improvement retailers, specialized veneer or joinery suppliers and kitchen suppliers.

Cost: ❹ High, but varies depending on the wood.

Specifications: Generally available 2 ft (600 mm) or 3 ft (900 mm) wide, and in lengths of 39 in (1,000 mm), 6½ ft (2,000 mm) or 10 ft (3,000 mm). Sheet thicknesses are about ⅞–1½ in (22–40 mm).

STRIP LAMINATES

Strip laminating is the process of resawing thick sections of lumber into thin strips and then reassembling them, either flat or clamped into shaped forms, by gluing them together under pressure. Strip laminates can be steamed into different shapes using a mold, or made to order by a joiner or furniture-maker, and can be used imaginatively to form colored or curved elements for furniture and cabinetmaking.

Properties: Strip laminates are easy to make into flexible and strong shapes, and are an ideal material for forms that would be brittle or wasteful if cut from solid wood. They are also used to vary the color or texture of surfaces by selecting a variety of woods and arranging them in layers. They make use of small sections of wood, as only the exposed surfaces must be intact to preserve structural integrity. Strength and texture are dependent on the species selected.

Use and Maintenance: Strip laminate is usually produced for specific purposes, such as curved sections for furniture or specialist veneers for countertop edges. When formed from a variety of materials, the attractive end grain can be used as trim (or nosing) for shelves, countertops and paneling. Exposed ends will require sanding and sealing to produce a smooth, durable seal. Because of its capacity for bending, strip laminate has many applications in furniture-making, creating free-form shapes or smooth, curved pieces. As with all wood products, laminates should be sealed on all sides to prolong life and prevent discoloring. Appropriate sealants are dependent on the type of wood used and its purpose. Care and maintenance depends in turn on the sealant or finish.

Safety and Environment: The raw materials used to make strip laminates should be produced from logs that are harvested from managed forests and will bear the mark of a certification body.

Availability: Strip laminates are specially made to your requirements. The raw materials and veneers are available from lumberyards and specialized joinery suppliers.

Cost: ❹–❺ High to very high, depending on the type of lumber used and the complexity of the component.

Specifications: Can take a wide variety of forms to suit specific purposes or designs.

LAMINATED FLOORING

This is a composite flooring material in which only the top layer is made of hardwood. Laminated boards provide a less expensive and more stable product than solid hardwood floorboards, and make available exotic woods that would otherwise be impractical or prohibitively expensive. This is a very uniform and easily installed product, which has the same warm, natural quality as hardwood flooring.

Properties: Laminated flooring is manufactured from sheets of cross-laminated lumber, pressure-bonded under heat with waterproof resin adhesive. Layer thicknesses and wood types vary, but general construction is a hardwood top layer, pine sheet on the bottom and spruce or fir strips sandwiched in the middle (arranged at right angles to the top). Selected hardwoods range from the familiar (beech, birch, oak, maple) to the exotic (merbau, zebrano, bamboo). Boards are either "single strip" (covered with one piece of veneer for a plank effect) or "multi-strip" (each clad with several staggered strips), and have a durable varnish finish on top and, usually, tongue and groove (see page 17) to all sides. Due to cross-bonding and reduced moisture sensitivity, laminate flooring is more stable than solid hardwood.

Use and Maintenance: Hardwood laminated flooring provides a natural, hard-wearing floor with a dependable performance, both in appearance and longevity. Specific types are designated for wet areas. Factory finishes are durable, easy to clean and extend the hardwood's life. They also mean no additional finishing is required and make laying straightforward and cost-effective. Flooring should be clipped or nailed to a subfloor, rather than fixed directly across joists. If the floor is damaged, or the finish eventually wears away, the surface can be sanded down and refinished.

Safety and Environment: Manufactured by large companies using certified lumber from sustainably managed sources. The finished flooring is safe and hygienic to live with.

Availability: From home-improvement retailers, lumberyards and flooring and carpet stores. Matching hardwood sections (such as thresholds) are also available.

Cost: ❷–❹ Low to high, depending on quality, thickness and durability of surface finish.

Specifications: Varying thicknesses, about ½–⅞ in (12–22 mm).
Board size is dependent on whether the top layer is single- or multi-strip.

WOOD • RUBBER, PLASTIC, RESIN & SYNTHETIC • METAL • GLASS • FABRIC • PAPER • LEATHER • PAINT, VARNISH & LACQUER • STONE, CERAMICS & TILES • CONCRETE & CEMENT • PLASTER

MELAMINE-COATED WOOD

INTERIOR MATERIALS & SURFACES: THE COMPLETE GUIDE

MELAMINE-COATED WOOD

This material features a decorative, durable plastic layer that is adhered to stable, inexpensive lumber. It is used for kitchen and bathroom counters and backsplashes, shelving and cabinetry. As well as utilitarian waterproof surfaces, which are practical and easily cleaned, melamine can be printed with decorative photographic effects to create the appearance of a more costly substance, such as steel or marble.

Properties: Melamine is a thermosetting plastic that can have a matte, textured or high-gloss finish. It is lightweight, strong in tension, and hard and brittle. It must be used adhered to a smooth backing substrate such as chipboard or MDF (see pages 21 and 35), or any sheet material. When applying laminate to a lumber substrate a balancing laminate must be applied to the opposite side or the sheet will curl. It can provide a bland finish for cabinet or ready-to-assemble furniture carcassing, or more vibrant surface textures and colors are available for kitchen or bedroom cupboard doors or shelves. There is a choice of hundreds of colors, patterns, textures and laminate finishes, although only a limited number appear on prefabricated items.

Use and Maintenance: Melamine is usually marketed as a cost-effective material for kitchen or bathroom counters or backsplashes. In order to saw melamine-coated wood sheets without chipping the surface, score first with a sharp blade. Melamine is susceptible to scratching and can crack or chip under a hard or sharp impact, but is generally resistant to staining. Splashes of boiling water will not damage the surface, but prolonged exposure to high temperatures will soften and distort it. Clean melamine with detergents or cream cleansers — never use abrasive pads. Dark stains may be removed with bleach.

Safety and Environment: Most wood bases are produced from logs that have been harvested from managed forests without wastage and will bear the mark of a certification body.

Availability: Countertops and shelving are available at lumberyards, home-improvement retailers and kitchen suppliers. Special laminates and variable boards can be ordered from lumberyards or building centers, fabricated to your requirements.

Cost: ❷–❸ Low to medium, depending on finish.

Specifications: Countertop widths 2 ft (600 mm) and 3 ft (900 mm); lengths 8 ft (2,440 mm) or 10 ft (3,000 mm), with varying thicknesses, 1¼–1½ in (30–40 mm). Other products vary according to use.

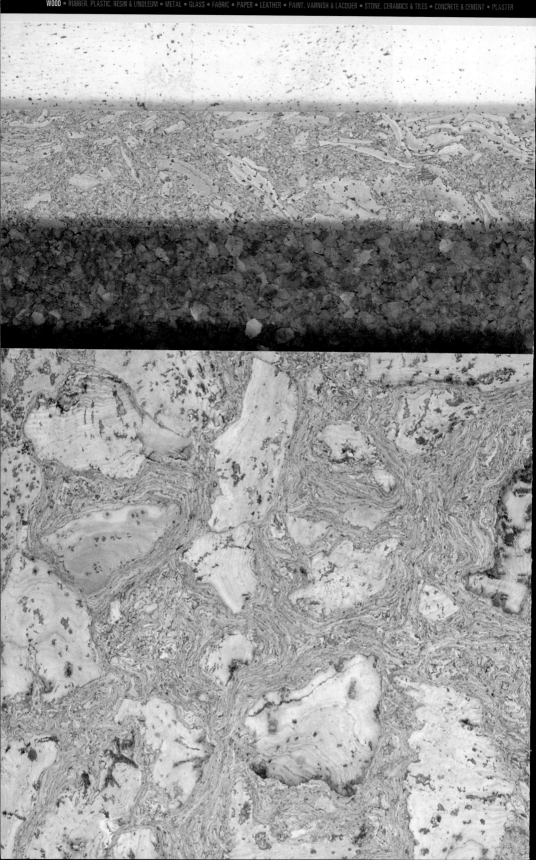

CORK

Cork oaks grow naturally throughout Europe and Asia, but those from the Mediterranean region are generally thought to have the most stable growth and produce the best-quality commercial-grade cork. Cork is the tree's bark, harvested and used in its raw form. It has a distinctive honeycomb texture and is one of the most versatile and durable of natural wood materials. It has a wide range of applications.

Properties: Cork has a fine elastic structure of tiny air pockets, making it very lightweight. It is resistant to extreme temperatures, molds easily to various shapes and reflects both heat and sound, so it has a high acoustic- and heat-insulation value. It is tough and long-lasting, but also nontoxic, soft and warm. It is resilient to water and impact damage and will not absorb dust. Its versatility has made it sought after for many commercial uses, from bottle stoppers to heatproof table mats to platform soles for shoes, as well as a variety of applications in the home.

Use and Maintenance: As a flooring, cork is very durable and provides a warm, soft and sanitary surface underfoot, and its elastic quality makes it comfortable to stand on for long periods. Since it is resistant to water, cork is also a suitable material for use in bathroom areas. Floor tiles should be adhered to a subfloor and sealed with specialized cork varnishes or oils (which will help prolong the surface appearance). Cork is also used as a compressible expansion strip around the perimeter of floating wood floors (broader across the end grains to allow for the extra potential expansion lengthwise). Cork tiles can also be adhered to walls for a paneling effect or to reduce noise and generate a feeling of warmth.

Safety and Environment: Cork is the most environmentally friendly wood product, having many certified suppliers. Stripped trees regrow their bark within ten years.

Availability: Cork tiles can be purchased from home-improvement retailers, flooring stores or building suppliers. Cork sheet (for pinboards, etc.) is available as a veneer from lumberyards and specialized joinery suppliers.

Cost: ❷ Low.

Specifications: Tiles for floors or walls are available unsealed or prefinished in standard sizes, most commonly 12 x 12 in (30 x 30 cm).

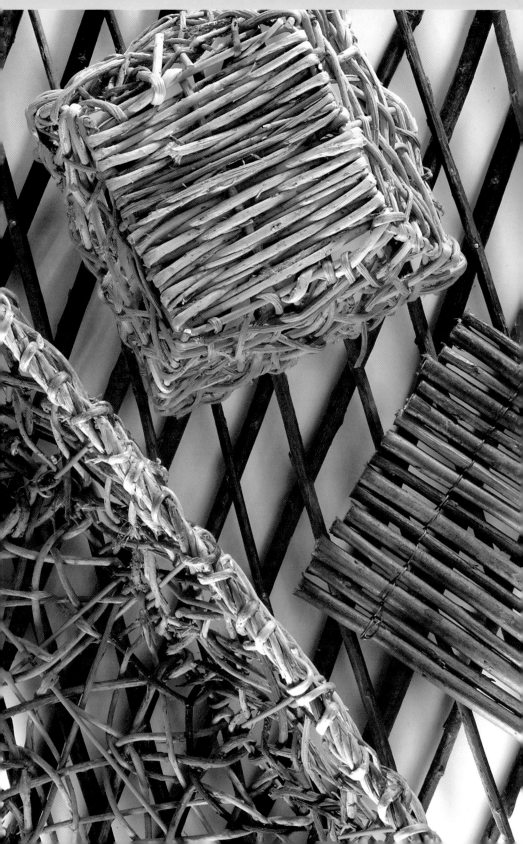

WILLOW

Willows are commercially grown in damp areas of the southern United States, particularly along the Mississippi, and the southern regions of northern Europe. It is one of the softer hardwoods and can be sawed, milled and cured as lumber, but trees are also specifically pruned (pollarded) to produce a mass of whippy stems, called withes, that are harvested for weaving.

Properties: Willow is not very useful as a structural material, as it is irregular and splits under compression, but it is easy to work with and therefore suited for handmade furniture, toys and utensils. The wood is susceptible to atmospheric moisture, but stable once dry. Its texture is fine and even with a straight grain. Color varies from creamy sapwood to reddish or grayish brown heartwood. Willow is easily worked and connected (with nails, screws or glue), and it sands to a smooth finish, but will not withstand bending, compression, stiffness or impact. As with all woods, willow is flammable; its fire rating depends on the sealants used.

Use and Maintenance: Willow lumber is used for furniture, doors, paneling and sports equipment. It can be whittled or carved and should be sealed with varnish or oil. Veneers can be used to cover screens or walls, or on sheets for shelves. Clean as per the requirements of the sealant. Use branches indoors for weaving into furniture, baskets and light fixtures, or for unadorned decorations and displays. Live branches and stems can be woven into backyard or playground structures, such as tepees and fences. They continue to grow, making a wonderful year-round feature (but do need annual pruning and training).

Safety and Environment: Willow trees grow efficiently and are a completely renewable resource.

Availability: Although willow lumber is produced in sufficient abundance, it is not a commonly used wood. It is therefore not widely stocked, but can be ordered from specialized lumber suppliers. Willow stems are available in garden centers and from specialized craft suppliers.

Cost: ❸ Medium.

Specifications: Lumber available in a limited range of standard and special sizes and lengths. Stems sold in bundles, either green (live), brown (dried with bark) or buff (dried, boiled and stripped).

MDF

MDF is an abbreviation for medium-density fiberboard. It is a cost-effective sheet material made up of fine wood particles bonded to produce a uniform wood product that is easy to work with and that has a smooth surface especially well-suited to paint finishes. It is suited to both handmade carpentry and the manufacture of high-tech, mass-produced items.

Properties: Fine wood fibers are pressure- and heat-bonded with synthetic resin adhesives into a flat, rigid, knot-free sheet. Its smooth, grain-free surface is ideal for veneers, laminates or specialist paintwork. It is also very dense, so thicker sheets are extremely heavy. MDF can be cut, drilled and filed with hand tools or machine tools, but it blunts tools quickly due to its high glue content. Its fine-grain sawdust is easily inhaled, so always work in a ventilated area using a mask and goggles. Pieces can be joined with nails, screws, carpenter's glue or dowels. MDF is susceptible to moisture, swelling and breaking down; even treated waterproof grades perform poorly in very wet conditions.

Use and Maintenance: MDF is mainly used for frameworks or in cabinets as wall panels and storage units. It is available in sheets or moldings, such as baseboards, and trim. Thinner, prescored (grooved) pieces, known as bendy MDF, are available for use on curved units. Because MDF releases urea-formaldehyde, all surfaces must be sealed with paint or varnish (wax or oil will not do). It takes both oil- and water-based paints and varnishes, but requires an undercoat to prevent absorption. Cut edges are even more thirsty than faces, so require sanding and extra coats.

Safety and Environment: The production of MDF makes use of small lumber offcuts that would otherwise be wasted. However, the urea-formaldehyde it continuously releases makes MDF a toxic product — both during processing and once in place — so take care while working with it and in finishing to reduce the danger. In some countries its use is discouraged.

Availability: Both sheets and moldings are widely available at lumberyards and home-improvement retailers.

Cost: ❷ Low.

Specifications: Standard sheet 4 x 8 ft (1,220 x 2,440 mm) in thicknesses ⅙–1 in (4–25 mm). Some are up to 4 x 10 ft (1,220 x 3,000 mm), or have thicknesses less or greater than standard.

VENEER

Veneers are thin layers of wood — often from exotic or expensive species — that can be used decoratively in fine woodworking or attached with adhesive to a backing board to form large sheets. Veneering as a process has been widely used in many cultures for over 3,000 years — the Egyptians, for instance, used veneers in furniture-making and to form pictures and patterns in marquetry.

Properties: Veneers are formed by turning a log against a lathe to slice off a thin continuous layer. This is arranged in consecutive bundles, then spliced together to form uniform sheets. Many species, around 170, are available in various patterns. Patterns include: herringbone, book matching (a repeated series of pairs), center matching (arranged around a center line), random matched (dissimilar sections in a planking format) and plain or flat cut (evenly arranged grains in a repeating V shape). Before it is adhered to a backing board, veneer is extremely brittle and fragile.

Use and Maintenance: Veneer can provide the look of expensive lumber without its cost or limitations. It is suitable for fine furniture, doors, closets and shelves. Some veneers are supplied with paper backing (known as 10 mil) or on flexible phenolic, when it is called laminate veneer. Veneers supplied adhered to a utility wood backer, such as chipboard or MDF, are called wood on wood.

Matching edgeband (a thin wood strip) is available to cover exposed edges. Raw or paper-backed veneers are suitable for marquetry or fine manufacturing. Veneer is fragile, so score with a sharp knife before sawing. Open-grain quality veneer is soft and easily damaged, so protect it with a hard varnish. Sand and reseal damaged veneer and clean in line with its sealant.

Safety and Environment: Sheets of veneer are produced without wastage from logs that have been harvested from managed forests. They will bear the mark of a certification body.

Availability: Lumberyards, building centers and specialized joinery suppliers stock veneers. Smaller craft sheets are also available from artists' materials stores.

Cost: ❸–❹ Medium to high, depending on the type of wood, pattern and backing material.

Specifications: A standard sheet, 4 x 8 ft (1,220 x 2,440 mm), available on a variety of backing materials. Small sheets are packaged for craft use.

WOOD • RUBBER, PLASTIC, RESIN & LINOLEUM • METAL • GLASS • FABRIC • PAPER • LEATHER • PAINT, VARNISH & LACQUER • STONE, CERAMICS & TILES • CONCRETE & CEMENT • PLASTER

HARDBOARD

INTERIOR MATERIALS & SURFACES: THE COMPLETE GUIDE

HARDBOARD

Hardboard is an inexpensive utility sheet material, available in a variety of thicknesses and textures. It has a slightly shiny finished surface on one side only and is often used as facing for flush (flat-faced) doors or for panels set within a wooden frame. It has many applications where the strength and durability of plywood (see page 19) are not required.

Properties: This material is manufactured from fine wood fibers extracted from wood chips and pulped wood waste that are heated and pressure-bonded with synthetic resin adhesives. It is even, flat and rigid. One side is grainless and smooth with a glossy finish; the back is textured. Hardboard is available in standard, flame-retardant or oil-tempered grades (to increase stiffness). It can be cut, drilled and filed using hand tools or machinery, and is stiff rather than strong.

Use and Maintenance: Its fine wood particles make hardboard a uniform material that is easy to work with in hand carpentry or mass production. Sheets with pressed, embossed or perforated patterns are available for specific uses, such as decorative radiator grilles. Surface-treated sheets (for wall paneling) also exist. It is often used as a substrate for melamine or wood veneers, but also makes an excellent base for specialist and decorative paintwork. Although it will take oil- or water-based paints and varnishes, it is highly absorbent, so requires a good undercoat. Hardboard is most useful as a temporary template, where a lightweight but rigid product is needed to help set out a pattern, or as an inexpensive protective cover for wooden floors when moving furniture. All grades (except treated ones) are susceptible to moisture, becoming waterlogged before swelling and breaking down.

Safety and Environment: The manufacturing process of this material makes use of small offcuts of lumber that would otherwise be wasted.

Availability: Easily sourced in sheet form from lumberyards or home-improvement retailers.

Cost: ❶ Very low.

Specifications: Standard sheet 4 x 8 ft (1,220 x 2,440 mm) available in incremental thicknesses, ½–¼ in (2–6 mm). Perforated or textured sheets of the same dimensions are slightly thicker.

RUBBER, PLASTIC, RESIN & LINOLEUM

Since Christopher Columbus sailed the Atlantic and opened up access to South America and its rubber trees, rubber has been used to waterproof seafaring vessels and manufacture footwear. However, unprocessed rubber, obtained by tapping the trees for their milky latex, remained sticky and had a low heat tolerance. It wasn't until the end of the 19th century that Charles Goodyear overcame these limitations by vulcanization, the process of mixing rubber with sulfur and charring at a high temperature, which transformed it into a highly useful plastic and elastic material. Demand for rubber escalated: every tire, hose, seal, gasket, valve and length of electrical wiring required this supple substance.

Rubber tree plantations sprang up throughout the tropics, notably in South America and Malaya, but with the market so reliant on a vulnerable natural material, the development in the 20th century of synthetic rubber was inevitable, and by 1964 synthetic rubber had garnered nearly half the world's rubber market. The synthetic material, however, is more expensive to produce than natural rubber, and is not strong enough for many uses, so natural rubber continues to be the main source of material in the production of most rubber products.

The development of synthetic rubber opened the field to a wide range of new synthetic materials, largely petrochemical byproducts. The first rubber replacement product,

parkesine, was developed in 1862. Soon afterward collodion was developed, to replace the ivory used in making billiard balls, leading to the creation of celluloid — a substance that could be used as a flexible photographic film. Both of these products are early examples of thermoplastics: materials that are melted and molded at high temperatures, retaining their shape when cooled, but melting again when heat is reintroduced. Then in 1907 Bakelite was developed. This liquid resin could be poured into a mold and, when set, would remain completely stable. It was extremely hard and would not burn, boil, melt or dissolve. This was the first of a group of plastics known as thermosets: once set, they retain their shape and form in almost any circumstances.

Modern plastics are classified as either thermoplastics or thermoset plastics and are produced for a myriad of different uses, from solid, glasslike polycarbonate to clear, thin cellophane sheet and film. Today's building industry and all our homes have profited from technology that has created plastics that can be exceedingly strong and resilient, porous but waterproof, fire-resistant, easily cleaned, inexpensive and long-lasting.

Plastics are continually being developed and refined, and some new and attractive products are emerging all the time. There are also interesting products being developed in specific response to the need to recycle plastics.

THERMOPLASTIC

Thermoplastic is a large family of synthetic petrochemical-based materials that are pliable and can be pulled, pressed or cast into shapes for numerous household and industrial uses. They include vinyls, polyethylene, polypropylene, polyesters and other plastics, and have many domestic applications, from coating electric wires to easy-clean floorcoverings and wallcoverings.

Properties: Thermoplastics are pliable, easily shaped and molded. Different plastics can be hard or soft at the same temperature depending on what is known as their Tg (glass transition temperature) — the temperature below which they are hard and brittle and above which they are soft and pliable. Additives can alter properties and Tg. Polyethylene is the most common thermoplastic; polypropylene is easy to produce in various colors and used cast or as fiber; polyester is produced as fibers or sheets. Plastics stretch when pulled, so are weak in tension. Thermoplastics are not damaged by water or sunlight.

Use and Maintenance: Polyethylene is usually sold in thin, translucent sheets for water- or wind-proofing. It can be extremely strong and is used as a permanent underlay as well as temporary protection (over drying concrete, for instance). Cast polypropylene makes colorful storage containers and can be opaque or translucent; as a fiber it forms artificial turf. Polyester fibers are woven into cloth, either alone or in combination with natural fibers (see Cotton, page 103). Polycarbonate or acrylic is a shatterproof alternative to glass (see page 88). Vinyl is widely used in either tile or sheet form as a floorcovering; it is resilient and warm underfoot, especially if cushioned. Wallcoverings for shower areas or backsplashes are also available, often textured and patterned to mimic tiling.

Safety and Environment: Thermoplastics are chemical preparations and do not biodegrade.

Availability: Buy from building suppliers, home-improvement retailers, garden centers, department stores and furniture stores.

Cost: ❷ Low.

Specifications: Available as building materials for use in plumbing, drainage, siding or insulation, or formed into numerous everyday products for packaging, toys and furniture.

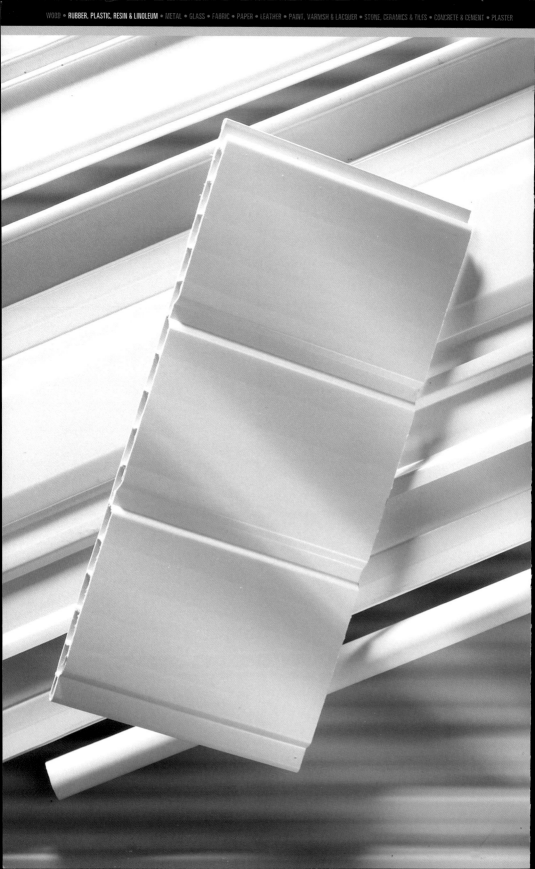

WOOD • **RUBBER, PLASTIC, RESIN & LINOLEUM** • METAL • GLASS • FABRIC • PAPER • LEATHER • PAINT, VARNISH & LACQUER • STONE, CERAMICS & TILES • CONCRETE & CEMENT • PLASTER

INTERIOR MATERIALS & SURFACES: THE COMPLETE GUIDE

VINYL

VINYL

Vinyl — or unplasticized polyvinyl chloride (also known as PVC) — is a synthetic material, originally used as a substitute for natural rubber. It is similar to polyethylene, being petrochemical-based, but has chlorine added. More than 50 percent of manufactured PVC becomes building products, replacing expensive raw materials with prefabricated components, from guttering and piping to window frames and siding.

Properties: The chlorine in PVC gives it two advantages over polyethylene: chlorine is a readily available, inexpensive commodity, making it less vulnerable to price fluctuations in the oil market. Secondly, when exposed to flame or high temperatures, it releases chlorine gas, an excellent flame retardant, so PVC products are highly resistant to ignition and flame spread (useful for electrical installations). Vinyl is a smooth, rigid thermoplastic, but added plasticizers soften and increase flexibility. Vinyl is resistant to acids and alkalis, and is the only plastic that can be thick or thin, flexible or rigid, delicate or tough, clear, opaque or colored. It is lightweight and tough at room temperature, and is smooth, stable, easy to clean and wear-resistant, although it can be scratched or gouged.

Use and Maintenance: Vinyl is used for fabricating many products in daily use in the building industry. It replaces wood as moldings, baseboards, doors and door frames, and draftproof frames for storm windows. It replaces copper, lead, brass and aluminum in plumbing, drainage and rainwater pipes, and has the advantages of resisting corrosion, sediment buildup and harsh, wet conditions. It has also replaced metal and rubber in components and wiring, as it insulates and lasts longer. Vinyl is also used to manufacture shower rails and drapes, siding, flooring and swimming pool liners.

Safety and Environment: Work-related diseases historically associated with the production of vinyls are mostly now prevented by improved manufacturing processes. PVC does not break down in landfill sites, but increasingly products are being recycled and made from recycled materials.

Availability: Various components from building suppliers, home-improvement retailers or electrical and plumbing suppliers.

Cost: ❷ Low.

Specifications: Wide variety of finished products for building materials and everyday use.

SHEET RUBBER

Rubber is derived from latex, a milky fluid tapped from trees (most often the tropical tree *Hevea brasiliensis*), although synthetic rubbers and additives have replaced natural rubber in many products. In the home, rubber is gaining popularity as a high-performance, long-lasting flooring material. It is available in a wide range of textures and colors, including precision-cut, computer-generated designs in several colors.

Properties: Most sheets are synthetic rubbers (elastomers), developed by the petrochemical industry. Synthetic rubber alters when exposed to high temperatures, but is burn- and scorch-resistant, waterproof, airtight and will not shrink or expand when properly adhered. Sheet rubber is homogeneous in construction, with no separate surface to wear off, and it does not fade or discolor. It resists dilute acids and alkalis, saline conditions and moisture. It is rotproof, antibacterial, antistatic and can be treated with extra fire retardant or for oil resistance. Rubber absorbs impact sound. It is antislip, resilient and cushioning, reducing leg fatigue.

Use and Maintenance: Sheet rubber comes in plain colors, geometric designs or patterns imitating materials such as wood, marble or terrazzo. It can also be embossed or textured, and computer etching can create all kinds of complex inlaid designs. It can be used over underfloor heating. Magnetic floor tiles are available for metallic access floors. Some rubber is suitable for outdoor use, for roof terraces or decks; take care choosing the surface and preparing the substrate. Rubber's density makes it heavy compared to linoleum or carpet. Use adhesive to install. Rubber does not require any sealing or seam welding at joints. On walls, use only specially produced thin sheets, as standard thicknesses will droop and crease. Keep dust- and grit-free. Wash with soapy water. Polish periodically to retain original sheen.

Safety and Environment: Some products are made from recycled materials. The proportion of synthetic to natural rubber produced is slightly more than 60 percent and there may well be a reversion to primary use of the natural product.

Availability: From flooring suppliers, building suppliers and home-improvement retailers.

Cost: ❸ Medium.

Specifications: Over 30 textures and 60 colors. Floor sheets: ¹⁄₁₀, ¹²⁄₁₀₀ or ³⁄₁₆ in (2.5, 3.2 or 4.8 mm) thick. Tiles: 12–27 in (305–680 mm) square to match all except greatest sheet thickness.

OILCLOTH

Oilcloth has been in use for over a hundred years. Originally it was used as an essential waterproof fabric for everything from flooring to clothing and wagon covers, and then as a decorative, wipe-clean tablecloth. Early oilcloths had a resin coating, which often cracked or flaked, but new oilcloth is coated with high-tech vinyl to provide a supple, durable waterproof material.

Properties: Floorcloths were made of heavy canvas, jute or burlap, sized with glue and coated with oil paints before going through various printing, varnishing and rolling processes. Today linoleum has replaced floorcloths, so oilcloth is manufactured from finer woven cotton fabrics (or flannel), coated with PVC vinyl (see page 45). It is impermeable to water. The cotton mesh backing makes it easy to cut with scissors and sew with a sewing machine (seal seams with silicone glue). It does not rip or tear and edges do not fray, so hemming is unnecessary. It is stain- and soil-resistant, durable and wipes clean.

Use and Maintenance: Oilcloth is valued for its vibrant colors (gingham and floral patterns are common) and traditional designs — some companies use original printing rollers — often featuring animal and wood prints. Its waterproof properties make it ideal for outdoor tablecloths, placemats, canopies, awnings, cushion covers and chair seats. Indoors, it is both decorative and practical, as protective tablecloths for craft activities, wipeable kitchen drapes and lampshades, upholstery, drawer liners and covering for cardboard boxes and wastebaskets. Black and green chalk cloth are produced for use as chalkboard vinyl (erasable and reusable). Hand-wash at low temperatures, ironing only on the reverse at a constant steam setting. Store folded (rather than rolled), allowing fold creases to relax out.

Safety and Environment: These fabrics are nontoxic, but vinyl does not biodegrade. It is not easy to recycle this mixed material, so it should be reused.

Availability: From fabric and department stores.

Cost: ❷ Low.

Specifications: Standard rolls: 48 in x 35 ft (122 cm x 10.8 m). Also as ready-made household products (aprons, awnings, tablecloths, etc.).

EPOXY RESIN

Epoxy resin is an excellent adhesive for joining different materials and is used where an extremely hard, weatherproof finish is required. Application is a two-part process: two measures of resin are mixed on site with one measure of hardener, creating a solid, strong material for bonding or filling. When modified with fillers, it effectively patches gaps and bridges voids, for instance on the bodywork of airplanes, cars and boats.

Properties: This high-performance product outperforms polyester resin in adhesion, weatherproofing and durability. It flows well and self-levels before setting, curing to a very hard, clear finish that can be sanded and shaped. It is chemical-resistant, resisting diesel and aviation fuel, but not gasoline (unless specially formulated). It resists sunlight and moisture, and is suitable for use with wood, glass, fiberglass, cement and various metals. It does not bond to most plastics, including polyethylene, polycarbonate, polyester fabrics or films. Ideally, epoxy resin should be applied between 53°F and 77°F (12°C and 25°C), for malleability and optimum curing time. It should not be stored at low temperatures.

Use and Maintenance: Epoxy resin is an excellent adhesive that can be used on bare or stained wood and is ideal for laminating curved lumber strips. Resin and hardener must be used at the same temperature; mix together for two minutes before applying. Lightly press components together during curing to avoid any movement. Epoxy resin is ideal for filling in chips or dents on highly trafficked wood. When using to fill or repair, it can be used alone or in conjunction with fiberglass mats (see page 57). Clean uncured product from tools with appropriate solvent cleaners; cured product must be removed with a combination of methylene chloride stripper, heating and scraping. Unmixed compounds can be cleaned up with white vinegar.

Safety and Environment: Epoxy resins can be harmful to skin and eyes or if inhaled. Use in a ventilated environment. Products are intended to weather well, so do not break down in sunlight and are difficult to recycle. Waste should be disposed of by special arrangement.

Availability: From building suppliers, boat or auto parts suppliers and home-improvement retailers.

Cost: ❹ High.

Specifications: Various types for specific purposes. Supplied in packs containing hardening catalyst. Sometimes supplied as a handy repair pack containing resin, hardener, fillers, tools, gloves and cleaners.

WOOD • RUBBER, PLASTIC, RESIN & LINOLEUM • METAL • GLASS • FABRIC • PAPER • LEATHER • PRINT, PATTERN & TEXTURE • STONE, CERAMIC & CONCRETE

LINOLEUM

INTERIOR MATERIALS & SURFACES: THE COMPLETE GUIDE

LINOLEUM

Linoleum is a flexible, man-made material traditionally used in sheet or tile form as a stable and low-maintenance floorcovering. It was once very popular, when inexpensive wipe-clean flooring was a novelty, but came to be viewed as cheap, boring and old-fashioned. However, with the wide range of colors now available, and the technology to produce exciting, unique designs, it is experiencing a revival.

Properties: Linoleum has an integral finish that does not require varnish or waxing and is dense, resisting furniture and castor indents. Its flexibility allows it to curve with radii as small as $\frac{1}{10}$–$\frac{1}{4}$ inch (2.5–6 mm) (depending on thickness). It contributes to acoustic improvement by reducing impact sound and is extremely colorfast (varying slightly from color to color). Color is uniform throughout the depth of the material. Linoleum is fire-resistant and does not melt.

Use and Maintenance: Linoleum is for indoor use only, conventionally as a floorcovering. It must be laid on a stable, level, clean subfloor and should not be used in damp areas. Sheets can be supplied with coved forms, to make moldings around the perimeter, like baseboards. Computerized pattern transfer and cutting enable innumerable glorious designs to be created, fitting together different colors, jigsawlike, into patterns of any complexity. Linoleum also works well on tables, desks and benches, where a warm, durable, low-maintenance surface is required. It is suitable for laying over underfloor heating, but should not be used vertically as it is heavy and will sag. Clean with a dry duster or use a damp cloth to spot-clean discolored areas. Remove any discoloration or marks (for instance, a cigarette burn) by gently rubbing with fine sandpaper and then finishing with a new coat of polish.

Safety and Environment: A stable material, easy and safe to use, although very heavy to lift in large sections. Its production is environmentally aware, and all offcuts are recycled within the process.

Availability: From carpet and flooring stores, department stores and home-improvement retailers.

Cost: ❷ Low, but quality varies to suit a range of uses and price brackets. For linoleum, it is worth going to the upper end of the market.

Specifications: Available in sheets or tiles, $\frac{3}{100}$–$\frac{16}{100}$ in (2–4 mm) thick.

CLEAR POLYCARBONATE

This is a clear thermoplastic that is used as a shatterproof replacement for glass. It can also be formed into complicated shapes where glass would be desirable but is too fragile or expensive to use. The largest single window in the world — California's Monterey Bay Aquarium window — is made of a sheet of clear polycarbonate 18 feet (5.5 meters) wide and over 54 feet (16.5 meters) long.

Properties: This is one of the hardest, strongest thermoplastics. It is often clearer than glass, which can have a greenish tinge unless specifically optically clear — even at 13 inches (33 cm) thick, the Monterey Bay Aquarium window is perfectly transparent. It also maintains its rigidity over a large temperature range. Polycarbonate is stiff and highly impact-resistant (250 times more so than glass). It resists chemicals and has high resistance to heat, cold and stress. It is antistatic, has good electrical insulation and generally has low flammability. It can yellow in sunlight, but with proprietary UV protection it has excellent weatherability. Its surface strength is not as high as glass; some products can be scratched or etched.

Use and Maintenance: Large sheets make clear, curved panels for covered walkways, and lightweight corrugated panels are used for translucent roofs or panels for greenhouses and sunrooms. These sheets can be cut with a handsaw.

It can be formed into more complex shapes such as barrel vaults, domes or pyramids to provide shaped roof lights. Mirrored polycarbonate can be used to make durable visual effects and features in the backyard. Clear polycarbonate can transmit light through the edges or along the length of a tube or rod, for a fiber-optic effect, used in lighting installations.

Safety and Environment: Thermoplastics are chemical preparations and do not biodegrade, but can be recycled.

Availability: From building suppliers, home-improvement retailers, garden centers, department stores and furniture stores.

Cost: ❷–❹ Low to high.

Specifications: Standard: 4 x 8 ft (1,220 x 2,440 mm), up to ½ in (1.25 cm) thick. Corrugated: 6½–23 ft (2–7 m) long, 18 or 24 in (45 or 60 cm) wide, 1 in (2.5 cm) thick. Also preformed into shapes.

RUBBER, PLASTIC, RESIN & LINOLEUM · METAL · GLASS · FABRIC · PAPER · LEATHER · PAINT, VARNISH & LACQUER · STONE, CERAMICS & TILES · CONCRETE & CEMENT · PLASTER

FIBERGLASS

FIBERGLASS

To make fiberglass, tiny strands of glass are woven into mats creating a flexible, malleable material. As well as being used to reinforce the bodywork of sports or automobile equipment, fiberglass sheets are used to make items that need to be light-weight, tough and waterproof, such as bathtubs, and many outdoor features, such as preformed pool liners and cascades.

Properties: Fiberglass is produced by a spinning process in which molten fibers of silicon oxide (plus additional oxides) are pulled out through a nozzle. Different oxides and additives alter their properties; phenol, for instance, increases fire security and reduces brittleness (but also strength). Fiberglass is strong, lightweight and has good resistance to corrosion and temperature fluctuation. It is usually woven, held together with an emulsion binder to form mats that can be used as a manufacturing material or for patching. Mats are generally used in conjunction with polyester or epoxy resins, which dissolve the binding material and allow fibers to follow mold contours. These liquid resins are mixed on site and stay in place (even vertically), drying to a slightly translucent tint. Filler or metal powders and colored pigments can be added.

Use and Maintenance: Due to fiberglass's ability to stand up to the elements, it is used for many maintenance-free outdoor items, from pond liners and feature fountains to fencing. Fibers are easily molded into shapes and hardened with resin for repairing fiberglass bathtubs, sinks, automobiles and recreational equipment, or for forming new objects. Bandage strips are available for repairing roof trim fascias and fiberglass roofing panels. Surface tissue is an extremely fine fiber mat that can be applied to fiberglass work to disguise its coarse glass pattern.

Safety and Environment: Care should be taken with these products as both fiberglass and resins can be harmful to skin and eyes or if inhaled. They do not break down in sunlight and are difficult to recycle. Dispose of waste by special arrangement.

Availability: From building suppliers, boat or auto parts suppliers and home-improvement retailers.

Cost: ❷ Low.

Specifications: Mats: 36 in (90 cm) wide in various thicknesses.
Surface tissue rolls: 39 in (100 cm) wide.

HIGH-PRESSURE LAMINATES

These thin, durable plastic sheets, available in many textures and colors, are intended to be adhered to a supporting substrate. They are traditionally constructed from layers of craft or decorative paper impregnated with thermosetting synthetic resins and fused under heat and pressure. They provide a high-performance surface for use as kitchen and bathroom counters and backsplashes, shelving or cabinetry.

Properties: Laminates can have a matte, textured or high-gloss finish. They are lightweight, strong in tension and hard but brittle (breaking rather than curving). Real wood veneer or metal is sometimes used under hard-wearing melamine resin. Laminates are susceptible to scratching and can crack or chip when subject to hard, sharp impact. Splashes of boiling water will not damage the surface, but prolonged exposure to high temperatures will soften and distort it. They are flame-retardant and generally stain-resistant.

Use and Maintenance: Hundreds of colors, patterns, textures and finishes exist, but only a limited number are used on prefabricated items. Cabinets, ready-to-assemble furniture and carcassing usually have a plain, utilitarian laminate (see Melamine-Coated Wood, page 29); more vibrant or natural textures and colors are available for kitchen and bathroom backsplashes and countertops. Laminates should be adhered to a stable substrate, such as chipboard or MDF (available preformed as countertops). When laminating lumber, it is essential to laminate the reverse (with a balancing laminate) or the wood will distort. Matching or contrasting strips to cover visible edges of the substrate are available. Laminates can become marked, so use a cutting board on countertops. Clean with detergents or cream cleansers (never use abrasive pads). Dark fruit juice stains or dyes may be removed with bleach.

Safety and Environment: Laminates are safe, stable products and new products are being developed to make use of recycled laminates. Most substrates are biodegradable.

Availability: Countertops and shelving from building suppliers, home-improvement retailers and kitchen suppliers. Special laminates and variable boards can be ordered from lumberyards/building centers.

Cost: ❸ Medium.

Specifications: Sheets: 4 x 8 ft (1,220 x 2,440 mm). Prefabricated countertops: 24 or 36 in (600 or 900 mm) wide, 8 or 10 ft (2,400 or 3,000 mm) long, in varying thicknesses, 1¼–1½ in (30–40 mm).

SOLID SURFACING

Solid surfacing is a product that has been developed for use in conjunction with high-pressure decorative laminates (see page 59). It is designed to replace wooden substrates and usually enhances the wearing abilities of the laminate surface. Because it is a uniform color all the way through, it does not show wear and also has the advantage of providing an integral, attractive, self-colored edge.

Properties: This is a high-performance, homogeneous material made from cast resin with mineral fillers. It has a hard-wearing surface and a satin, gloss finish. This can be worked with a router or acid etching to vary the texture or produce inlaid effects. It is susceptible to scratching and can crack or chip under hard, sharp impact. Splashes of boiling water will not damage the surface, but prolonged exposure to high temperatures will soften and distort it. Solid surfacing is generally resistant to stains and chemicals. It is nonporous, nontoxic and hygienic.

Use and Maintenance: Wooden substrates are often softer than the laminate that covers them and either fail when exposed to demanding wear or are unattractive if the laminate wears through. Solid surfacing is a much harder, more durable material and, unlike laminated lumber, which is often let down by fragile or uninteresting nosing material, solid surfacing substrates do not need to be covered and are an integral feature. Solid surfacing is suitable for doors, cabinets, cubicles, kitchen and bathroom counters and screens. It also makes hygienic, hard-wearing wallcoverings. Sharp blades can mark laminates, so use a cutting board on countertops. Clean with detergents or cream cleansers (never use abrasive or scouring pads). Dark fruit juice stains or dyes may be removed with bleach.

Safety and Environment: Once in place, solid surfacing is nontoxic, but protective masks must be worn while cutting, sawing or sanding this material (because of the resin base). Solid surfacing is not biodegradable, but new products are being developed to use recycled material.

Availability: Sheets available, usually to order, from lumberyards, building suppliers, home-improvement retailers and kitchen suppliers.

Cost: ❹ High.

Specifications: Sheets: 4 x 8 ft (1,220 x 2,440 mm), either ¼, ½, ⅝ or ¾ in (6, 12, 15 or 20 mm) thick, in about 20 colors.

PLASTIC EXTRUSIONS

These are made by extruding or pressing heat-softened plastics through a mold to form strips of various sizes, thicknesses and shapes. As soon as a product can be identified and standardized, it can be designed and produced as an extruded plastic. A variety of thermoplastics are used, including PVCs or vinyl, polycarbonate, polyethylene, nylon and thermoplastic rubbers, to form prefabricated components.

Properties: Extruded plastics are formed by pressing malleable plastics through a metal die or form cut with wire cutters or laser machines. They can have limitless sizes and shapes (tubes, channels, angles, box sections), be rigid or flexible, thick or thin, delicate or tough, clear, opaque or colored. They are lightweight and tough at room temperature. They resist acids and alkalis and are smooth, stable, easy to clean and resistant to wear (but can be scratched or gouged). They also resist corrosion, sediment buildup and harsh, wet conditions. Their heat tolerance depends on the material used. Some are UV-resistant and suitable for outdoor use. Co-extrusions involve two different colors or types of plastic, extruded and fused together at the same time.

Use and Maintenance: More than 50 percent of thermoplastic extrusions produced are for use as prefabricated building products, replacing traditional materials that are more expensive or more difficult to use. They include window frame sections, doors and door frames, baseboards and drape tracks (especially for curved areas such as showers or bay windows). Extruded plastic pipe has replaced copper, lead, brass and aluminum for plumbing, drainage and rainwater pipes. Extrusions are used to make exterior vinyl sidings, fascias and building trims, suspended ceiling sections, stair nosings, ceramic tile trims, outdoor furniture and fence posts.

Safety and Environment: Some plastics do not break down in landfill sites, but more products are being recycled and made from recycled materials.

Availability: Windows, doors, moldings and building components from building, electrical and plumbing suppliers, and home-improvement retailers. Indoor and outdoor furniture from department stores and garden centers.

Cost: ❸ Medium.

Specifications: Many manufacturers make up shapes to special order.

METAL

One of the most significant developments in human civilization was the discovery and exploitation of naturally occurring metals, such as gold, copper and tin. The development of copper tools to replace stone, from around 2400 BCE, changed the way in which technology progressed. Later, in addition to being worked into useful tools, it was discovered that copper could be cast to create objects such as weapons, coins, pots, drinking vessels and jewelry. Gold was coveted for its untarnishable beauty and the ease with which it could be worked, but its rarity and comparative softness meant it was largely reserved for decoration.

The need for specific ideal conditions to process natural ores led to the development of alloys, where different metals are added to alter the properties of the original metal. Working copper required very high temperatures and it was discovered that the introduction of tin lowered the melting point, making it a much more usable material. This led to the discovery of bronze, the alloy of copper and tin, which was widely used for metalwork, and the Bronze Age transformed the direction of industrial development. Brass is a mixture of copper and zinc, extensively used by the Romans as an industrial metal because it was hard and noncorrosive. Copper, however, was relatively rare, while iron was abundant and comparatively easy to mine, and this became the metal of choice. Iron was

frequently mixed with other metals and when combined with carbon created steel. There is evidence of steel being made and used in China as early as 2550 BCE.

Steel is the main structural metal of today's construction industry. It comprises a large group of alloys and its properties can be varied with the addition of nickel, chromium and tungsten. Metals in general are valued for their flexibility, their high strength and the ease with which they can be worked with simple machinery. Copper and silver are important due to their ability to conduct electricity. Silver is also the most reflective of all metals and is used as a backing for glass in making mirrors. Many metals will rust or corrode in the atmosphere, but some, such as lead, zinc and brass, can be used as a covering to protect another metal, such as copper, from corrosion.

Metals can be used to perform a utilitarian structural or serviceable role, often unseen, but they are increasingly appreciated as a finishing surface in homes. Steel, copper and brass fixtures are becoming more widely available for rooms inside and out. And as sophisticated applications of high-carbon steel push the boundaries of the material ever further in superstructures such as bridges and skyscrapers, they inform the way we use metal in our homes, as we make features of steel staircases and exposed structural metal girders, columns and brackets.

WOOD • RUBBER, PLASTIC, RESIN & LINOLEUM • **METAL** • GLASS • FABRIC • PAPER • LEATHER • PAINT, VARNISH & LACQUER • STONE, CERAMICS & TILES • CONCRETE & CEMENT • PLASTER

IRON, FORGED AND WROUGHT

INTERIOR MATERIALS & SURFACES: THE COMPLETE GUIDE

IRON, FORGED AND WROUGHT

Iron made malleable by the heat of a fire, then hammered and wrought (bent) into shape is often seen in decorative fences and gates, especially on buildings dating back to the end of the 19th century, and is well known for withstanding corrosion. Today ironworking is mainly a decorative craft, but its skills are kept alive by artisans and the maintenance work required to upkeep existing installations.

Properties: Wrought iron is a mixture of near-pure iron with up to 5 percent noncorrodible glass slags. These form linear fibers in the metal, making it workable under high heat. It is not suitable for machining and is forged or handworked with hammer and anvil by a blacksmith. Wrought iron is not brittle, seldom breaks and is strong in tension and compression (stronger than cast iron, which is shaped by being melted and poured into a mold). Being handcrafted, it is expensive, but it is extremely long-lasting.

Use and Maintenance: The Romans used this as a structural building material, and in the Middle Ages wrought-iron lateral ties were used to retain the shape of masonry arches and domes. By the latter half of the 19th century it was widely used for bridges and train stations, but demand for ever-greater spans finally relegated it to ornamental use. Uses today are mainly decorative furnishings, accessories and security gates. It is perfect for outdoor furniture, and popular indoors for chairs, beds, drapery rails, light fixtures and door hardware. It is suitable for extremely fine work, but must be forged by a skilled blacksmith. Its low corrodibility can be enhanced by well-maintained paintwork. Monitor exterior ironwork regularly: clean and seal any rust (with particular attention to joints), and repaint thoroughly at least every five years.

Safety and Environment: This material is long-lasting and stable. The life of items far exceeds the energy required to produce them.

Availability: Due to the material's longevity, items often surface in salvage yards and antique stores. Customized items can be commissioned from skilled artisans. New off-the-rack items are generally made of cast iron, rather than wrought iron.

Cost: ❹ High.

Specifications: Dependent on the intended purpose or design.

MILD STEEL

Mild steel, also called low-carbon or soft-cast steel, is the most common type of steel used in construction. It is the modern replacement for wrought iron and can be seen in a range of manufactured items, from household appliances and utensils to building components and decorative claddings. It can be used untreated, or primed and painted (or stove enameled), and remains stable over a long lifespan.

Properties: Steel is an alloy of iron and carbon; mild steel contains only a tiny proportion of carbon (less than 0.25 percent), but can have other metals added, to create high-strength low-alloy steel (HSLA) — copper, for example, improves corrosion resistance, nickel surface quality and nitrogen strength and weldability. Mild steel is annealed (heated red-hot then cooled slowly) to improve workability and reduce its brittleness. Cor-ten steel oxidizes rapidly to a deep brown and resists corrosion. Mild steel can also be galvanized with zinc for a weatherproof finish (see page 83). It can be welded, cut, rolled, folded or bent into shape and maintains stability. Mild steel does not promote fire spread, but structural steel should be encased or painted with flameproof paint. It has high strength in tension and compression, and retains impact resistance at low temperatures.

Use and Maintenance: Due to superior strength and weldability, mild steel is mainly used for structural elements such as trusses, beams, lintels and posts. Specialized items can be fabricated. Perforated or sheets are available for screens or panels and tubes can be used for table legs. Other uses include staircases and safety nosings for stairs. Galvanized steel is used for outdoor furniture, planters, watering cans and grates for rainwater gulleys. Cor-ten is often chosen for sculptures because of its attractive color.

Safety and Environment: Mild steel's high strength means less material is needed, making its use efficient. New and old steel is 100 percent recyclable.

Availability: As a high level of prefabrication will be required, this material has to be sourced directly from a manufacturer (contact details can be sourced through building suppliers).

Cost: ❸ Medium.

Specifications: Available in many furnishings, fixtures and appliances. A wide range of rectangular, round and square tubes, rods and sheets are available from metal suppliers.

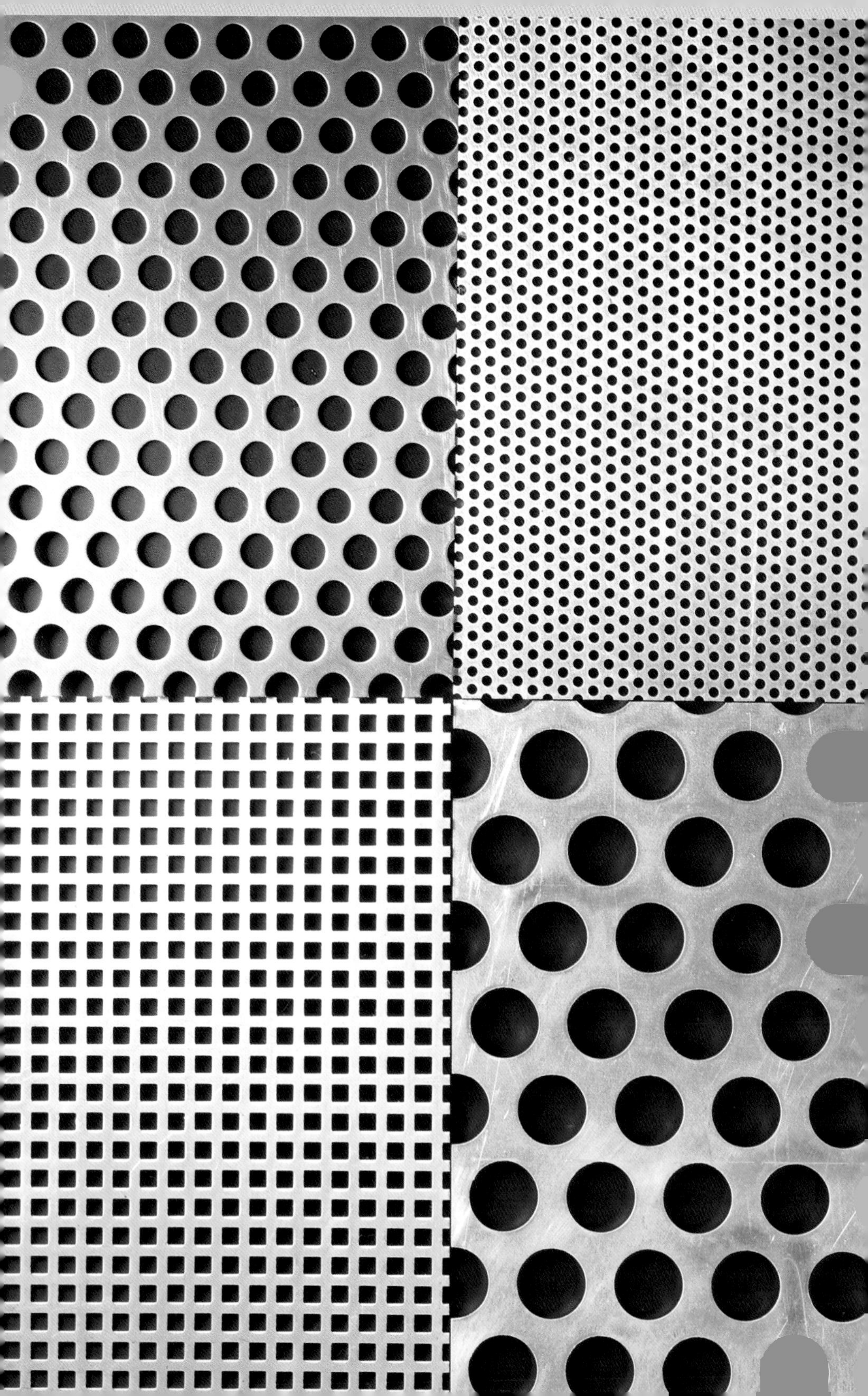

PUNCHED AND PIERCED SHEET METAL

Sheet metal can be punched, pierced, pressed or perforated in a variety of regular patterns. These perforated sheets have traditionally been used in industrial applications as components of, or cladding for, machinery or building materials. They can also be employed in a decorative function — individual items can be produced for specific purposes, fabricated by the supplier to exact requirements.

Properties: Standard sheets of metal (usually aluminum, stainless steel or brass) are perforated with a regular pattern, either to reduce the material's overall weight or to provide a texture or transparency above another material, altering the visibility. Perforated metal maintains stability when rolled, folded or bent into shapes (easily achievable with specialized equipment). It is resistant to water, steam and most chemicals, depending on the metal and surface treatment used. Perforation patterns that extend right to the perimeter of a panel often leave sharp edges that need to be rolled over or covered with metal edging or trim.

Use and Maintenance: Industrial design uses punched metal in a variety of applications, from grilles and decking to furniture. Many sheets can be factory-finished by polishing, or anodizing, or colored by a coating of stove enamel, and will not require further treatment. Sheets are used for decorative screens, wall panels, infill for balustrading, cupboard doors and light diffusers. When ordering a custom-made sheet, all the details of your requirements (including edge treatments) must be considered and agreed upon with the fabricator beforehand. Sheet metal is easy to maintain with a damp cloth, but finishes are susceptible to scratch damage or dents from high impact. It is generally hard-wearing and dents can be hammered out (although damage to the finish would remain).

Safety and Environment: Exposed edges are extremely sharp and dangerous during handling. They should never be left uncovered in the final installation. Metal products are ideal for recycling.

Availability: Because a high level of prefabrication is required, this material must be sourced directly from a manufacturer — building centers can supply contact details.

Cost: ❸ Medium.

Specifications: Sheets 1/50–3/8 in (0.5–9 mm) thick. Framing trims and channels in various styles. Finishes: anodized, polished (satin or bright), paint (stove enamel polyester powder coating; c. 60 colors).

WOVEN SHEET STEEL

Metals can be woven into meshes and cloths, which are available in a variety of sizes and patterns, effects and qualities, each achieved from different metals and different gauges. Heavy-duty weaves have many specific industrial applications (such as filters and screens), but both heavy and finer weaves are also highly attractive when used decoratively, either flat or sculpted into shapes.

Properties: Various steels and alloys are used to create woven metal, depending on whether such properties as heatproofing or fireproofing or a non-corrosive nature are needed. Different patterns available include the simple square mesh, with warp and shute (weft) wires, equally sized and spaced and making alternating passes; plain mesh, in which the warp wires are larger than the weft; and twill, in which each wire passes over two others. Wire cloth is pressed to reduce its thickness, providing a smooth surface. Fine metal strands are also woven with colored silk, creating a luxurious fabric for dressmaking and drapery.

Use and Maintenance: Fine mesh can be cut with shears or scissors, larger grades with wire snips. Medium mesh can be hung on walls or ceilings and used with hooks to hang tools and utensils. Heavy gauge mesh is suitable indoors or out, for screens, balustrading and trellises. Fine metal cloth can be sculpted into dramatic shapes for light shades or window coverings, or stretched flat or ruched for blinds and screens. Once handled, mesh (and cloth) retains creases, and only factory rerolling will restore absolute flatness. Whether a mesh will tarnish or corrode is dependent on the metals used, and maintenance depends on whether they are subject to water or chemicals, and whether any sealants have been used.

Safety and Environment: Exposed edges are extremely sharp and dangerous during handling. They should not be left uncovered in the final installation. Metal products are ideal for recycling.

Availability: Building centers stock large gauges. Fine gauges are sold by art suppliers in small sheets. Matching stitching and stapling wire exists (for joining mesh constructions). Metal fabric is available in fabric stores.

Cost: ❷–❹ Low to high.

Specifications: Available in full rolls or cut pieces, in grades from very fine to fairly heavy, and from micronic to 1 in (2.5 cm) openings, or up to 3 in (7.5 cm) for industrial applications.

COPPER

Copper has been mined for over 5,000 years and some of the earliest surviving metal tools and jewelry are made of it. It is a shiny, reddish metal, which develops a green or brown patina when exposed to water or chemicals. It is available in many shapes and forms, which are used for specific technical and decorative purposes, from plumbing pipes to high-quality pots and pans.

Properties: This material has a high capacity for conducting heat and electricity. It resists atmospheric corrosion (but will dissolve in nitric acid) and is nontoxic, malleable and easy to use. Copper will maintain stability when rolled, folded or bent into shapes, which is easily achieved with specialized equipment. It can be chemically treated to create a variety of finishes, such as bright or deep green or brown, or mottled or textured effects. Because of its softness, copper is not suitable as a structural material. It can be combined with numerous metals to form alloys and does not burn or support combustion.

Use and Maintenance: Copper pipes are extensively used in water and gas plumbing, and copper wiring in electric and electronic installations. As sheeting, copper is used for roofs — both for its functional weatherproofing quality and as a finishing material to highlight its natural beauty. It features in interior and exterior furniture, light fixtures, ironwork and ornamental crafts. It can also be used indoors in areas subject to heat, such as kitchen or fireplace hoods, counters and backsplashes, cookware and cutlery. It is suitable for wet applications too, including bathtubs, shower trays and basins, but use a sealant if you want to avoid tarnishing the pinkish red finish. It can be textured for a hammered or dimpled finish.

Safety and Environment: This metal can be recycled again and again, without losing any of its properties.

Availability: Available from metal suppliers in sheets or foil. Copper piping, wires, rods and so on are available from building suppliers.

Cost: ❹ High.

Specifications: Sheets are cut to order and sold by the meter. Thicknesses range from $\frac{1}{12}$–2 in (2–50 mm). Pipes, wire, rods, foil, ingots and many compounds (such as paints) are also available.

BRASS

For centuries brass has been used to make armor and religious monuments, owing to its rich, golden color. This metal was also used in the early production of precision instruments and clocks. Today brass is not usually available as a raw product, but is used rather for an almost infinite number of components or fixtures for practical and decorative use.

Properties: Brass is an alloy of copper, zinc, lead and tin, combined in different amounts for differing qualities. It is frequently used in plate form (for gilding), but can be very durable in engineering due to its ability to spring back rather than bend. Although noncorrosive, it develops a green patina if unsealed and exposed to moisture. It provides the perfect base for plating with chrome, gold or other metals, or for vitreous (baked) enameling. It conducts electricity, is nonmagnetic and can withstand high temperatures without softening, burning or supporting combustion.

Use and Maintenance: It is usually manufactured as industrial components or building materials such as piping, or finished products plated for a decorative finish or noncorrosive surface. Brass fixtures are available for indoor and outdoor use, including handles, locks, light fixtures, faucets and decorative objects. Brass is also used for fire surrounds and hearth tools. Perforated sheets make radiator grilles and panels for screens and cabinet doors. Thin sheets can be laser-etched with a pattern. Treat brass with a sealant to prevent it from tarnishing or greening. Colored patinas can be created by chemical treatments. Brass can be cleaned with polish or ultrasonic agitation. Plated brass gives a bright, smooth finish to ironwork and kitchen and bathroom fixtures. Vitreous enameled brass is used for jewelry, door handles and faucet tops.

Safety and Environment: Brass is actively collected and recycled, making it an environmentally friendly product.

Availability: Thin brass sheets for laser etching can be provided by an etching house. Brass, metal-plated and enamel-plated products and fixtures are available from a variety of retailers, as well as salvage yards and antique dealers.

Cost: ❸ Medium.

Specifications: Sheets ⅟₅₀ in (0.5 mm) thick are available for computer-controlled laser or acid etching, using a digital image. Brass is also available as plating for almost any metal object.

WOOD • RUBBER, PLASTIC, RESIN & LINOLEUM • **METAL** • GLASS • FABRIC • PAPER • LEATHER • PAINT, VARNISH & LACQUER • STONE, CERAMICS & TILES • CONCRETE & CEMENT • PLASTER

ALUMINUM

INTERIOR MATERIALS & SURFACES: THE COMPLETE GUIDE

ALUMINUM

This silvery white metal is usually available as a sheet, which can be rolled, pressed, perforated or woven in a variety of regular patterns, traditionally for use in industrial applications. It is widely used for ordinary household fixtures such as hooks and rails, as well as outdoor furniture, but its adaptability gives it potential for individually commissioned items, from chairs to garden sculptures.

Properties: Aluminum will maintain stability when rolled, folded or bent, easily achieved with specialized equipment. Its factory finish, whether polished, anodized or colored with stove enamel, means it does not require additional refinishing. It is resistant to water, steam and most chemicals, although abrasive cleansers cause damage. It will rust if left untreated, and can also be damaged by biometallic corrosion when exposed to copper, iron or steel (or products containing these metals). Aluminum may become discolored during the drying process of adjacent concrete, mortar or plaster. It neither burns nor supports combustion.

Use and Maintenance: This metal is widely used in industrial applications for building components such as gutters, grilles, siding and decking, as well as for furniture and other design products. It can be used for forming decorative screens, wall panels, infills, covers and light diffusers. When ordering a customized product, full details of your requirements must be agreed upon with the fabricator before going ahead, including the finish and type of edge treatment to be used. Edging options include rolling sharp edges over, or covering them with trim or frames. Aluminum is easy to maintain with a damp cloth, but finishes are susceptible to scratching. It is generally extremely hard-wearing, and dents can be hammered out smooth, but damage to the finish cannot be repaired in this way.

Safety and Environment: Exposed edges of aluminum sheeting are extremely sharp and dangerous during handling. They should not be left uncovered in the final installation.

Availability: This material will have to be sourced directly from a manufacturer — building suppliers will have contact details. Framing trim and channels are also available.

Cost: ❸ Medium.

Specifications: Sheets pressed, perforated or woven, in thicknesses ⅟₅₀–⅜ in (0.5–9 mm), depending on pattern. Finishes: anodized, polished or colored with stove enamel polyester powder coating.

STAINLESS STEEL

Familiar from its wide use for household appliances and fixtures, stainless steel's stability, resistance to corrosion and its even, lustrous finish make it the metal of choice for a great many serviceable uses — its qualities have long been appreciated in commercial kitchens. It also has great decorative potential, and its strength and durability make it suitable in the manufacture of structural components.

Properties: A low carbon steel that contains chromium, stainless steel is resistant to water and atmospheric corrosion. Certain grades even resist acids and chlorine. It has high strength in tension and compression, and is heat- and fire-resistant. It is also impact-resistant, even at low temperatures. Its strength allows it to be used in reduced thicknesses, making it very efficient in terms of the amount required. It can be welded, cut, rolled, folded and bent into shapes (using specialized equipment), and will maintain stability. It also remains stable over a long lifespan. Stainless steel is an integral material, so requires no sealant or added surface protection.

Use and Maintenance: Stainless steel does not deteriorate and requires no sealant or applied surface finish. Its regular, brushed look has a high-tech, modern feel. Its smooth surface is easy to wipe clean and perfect for areas requiring a high level of hygiene. It is used for indoor and outdoor products, including outdoor furniture, exterior light fixtures, household appliances and ironwork. New uses, such as wall tiles, are constantly being developed. Sheets can be used as backsplashes or formed into countertops with integral sinks, nosings and moldings. Sheets can also be used as paneling or to line wet areas, and as structural or decorative elements in garden design.

Safety and Environment: The high strength of this material makes for efficient use. New and old stainless steel is 100 percent recyclable.

Availability: Since it requires a high level of prefabrication, this material has to be sourced directly from a manufacturer (details can be found through building suppliers). An extensive range of rods, tubes and sheets can be sourced from metal suppliers.

Cost: ❹ High.

Specifications: Available in a wide range of furnishings, fixtures and appliances. For kitchen surfaces use sheets ½ in (2 mm) thick.

ZINC

This is a shiny white sheet metal with a bluish gray luster that deepens over time. Zinc's use as a countertop in French bars was once so ubiquitous that it has become synonymous with the bars themselves. However, zinc's many other qualities besides its invulnerability to wine and elbows has led to uses as varied as garden tools and ornaments and a protective coating for other metals.

Properties: Although brittle, zinc cuts easily and is malleable when slightly heated, which makes it suitable for working into complex, intricate shapes. It does not burn or support combustion and is insoluble in water, making it noncorrosive and salt-resistant. It is, however, soluble in acids and alkalis. Zinc is often used as a galvanizing material: thin layers of it are plated onto lead, iron or steel to give them a noncorrosive surface. It has a clean finish and is ruggedly durable.

Use and Maintenance: Zinc is used either as a pure sheet or cast material, as galvanizing for other metals or in compounds. Its waterproof quality makes it ideal outdoors, where it has a long, maintenance-free life in guttering, downpipes, roofing and siding. Galvanized products include garden tools, planters, furniture and railings. Indoors, it is particularly suitable for areas subject to water, such as bartops, kitchen counters and backsplashes; it makes a hygienic surface, but as it is not particularly hard and sharp, knives will mark it, so use a cutting board. Zinc basins are also available, and it is advisable, if choosing a deep, Japanese-style wooden bathtub, to have it zinc-lined; wood-only bathtubs, like barrels, will leak if not kept full of water.

Safety and Environment: Zinc can be recycled again and again without losing any of its properties. More than a third of all zinc products have been formed from reclaimed zinc.

Availability: Can be sourced from metal suppliers, and as a raw material or finished products from building centers, salvage yards and antique dealers.

Cost: ❸ Medium.

Specifications: Sheets cut to order and sold by length. Thicknesses ½–1 in (2–25 mm). It is also available as wire, rods, foil, powder, ingots and compounds.

WOOD • RUBBER, PLASTIC, RESIN & LINOLEUM • **METAL** • GLASS • FABRIC • PAPER • LEATHER • PAINT, VARNISH & LACQUER • STONE, CERAMICS & TILES • CONCRETE & CEMENT • PLASTER

LEAD

INTERIOR MATERIALS & SURFACES: THE COMPLETE GUIDE

LEAD

This is a matte, dark gray metal sheet material. It is soft, malleable and easily worked by hand, and has been used since ancient times for pipework and waterproofing — the Romans used it to line aqueducts and it is visible as the covering on complex domed roofs. Lead is found in many compounds. It is present in lead crystal, pottery glazes and some paints (although most are now discontinued).

Properties: Lead is extremely heavy, making it awkward to transport, but stable under high winds. Its density makes it useful in reducing vibrations and sound waves (and as a shield against x-rays, gamma rays and nuclear radiation). A buildup of lead in the body can be toxic, but although it was once common in plumbing systems, existing lead pipes will have developed limescale coatings (which reduce this effect); plumbers will prefer to replace old piping rather than join new copper to old lead. Lead is noncorrosive, so ideal for elementally exposed areas, but is subject to biometallic corrosion, so requires copper or stainless-steel fittings. Correctly installed, lead is maintenance-free and long-lasting. Although noncombustible, it has a low melting temperature of 621.3°F (327.4°C).

Use and Maintenance: It is usually used as sheets for waterproofing, guttering, flashing and covering uneven areas. Because it is so soft, it must be laid on a stiff substrate. Its deep, luminous color makes attractive panels. These can be used anywhere (including bathrooms), but will remain soft and prone to damage. Never use lead for a food preparation countertop. It is ideal outdoors, as plant container coverings, garden feature panels or part of a fountain. New lead will oxidize outdoors. This whiteness washes off in rain, staining adjacent materials. To avoid discoloration, treat with a solvent or water-based sealant.

Safety and Environment: If ingested or inhaled, lead is a cumulative poison, so wear protective gloves and a mask when handling the raw material. Used lead is recovered through an environmentally responsible active sourcing and recycling program.

Availability: From metal and building suppliers, and as raw material or finished products at salvage yards and antique dealers.

Cost: ❹ High.

Specifications: Sheets are cut to order and sold by the yard (meter). Thicknesses are $\frac{1}{12}$–1 in (2–25 mm). Lead is also available as wire, rods, foil, powder, ingots and many compounds.

GOLD LEAF

So thin as to be almost see-through, this fragile foil provides a finish with the brilliance of real gold (it can be either pure gold or a mixture of cheaper materials). Gilding, the ancient technique for covering complicated surfaces with this delicate foil (or gilt), can be seen on Italian art from the 14th century, picture frames and candelabras, and is used today in craft projects and restoration work.

Properties: Metal leaf highlights intricate shapes, but can reveal imperfections. Genuine gold leaf is hand-beaten 22- or 24-carat gold, but may contain copper or additional metals. White gold leaf is half silver, half gold. Genuine silver leaf contains no gold or alloys, edible gold leaf no copper. Gold leaf does not tarnish or dull, although it can rub off with wear. Leaf can be applied to a colored clay base layer to enhance or dull its effect: red makes it appear warmer; black reduces intensity (especially on protrusions); yellow lightens recessed areas.

Use and Maintenance: Leaf is intended as the finishing layer; varnish or seal can dull or discolor it. If using leaf outdoors, or where it would be subject to heavy wear, however, an appropriate varnish is necessary. Leaf can cover repairs, as it masks joints and textures. It takes to simple or complex wooden, plaster or stone shapes, provided they are prepared with a smooth, absorbent base coat (such as gesso). Its fragility requires knowledge and experience of proper, traditional use, but skills can be learned and no high-tech tools are required. It can be applied to picture frames, mirrors, screens, moldings or walls. Aligned leaves create a grid pattern, so overlap leaves if you want overall gilding.

Safety and Environment: Gold leafing uses small amounts of a precious metal that is processed by hand without any significant environmental impact. Some alloys are harmful if ingested.

Availability: From specialized art material suppliers as books of leaves (leaves are separated by tissue paper or attached to waxed paper) or in rolls.

Cost: ❺ Very high.

Specifications: Leaves 3½ x 3½ in (85 x 85 mm) square; rolls ⅛–4 in (3–100 mm) wide. Double gold is 10–20 percent thicker than regular sheets.

GLASS

Glass production is likely to have originated in Mesopotamia in 3000 BCE, where it was produced in chunks and used as precious jewels. By the time it reached ancient Egypt, the technique of wrapping molten glass over a form to create vessels and decorative objects had evolved. By the first century BCE, glass-blowing had developed in Syria. The Romans adopted this technique and the use of glass for decoration spread throughout their empire. The glass industry continued to grow in Mesopotamia and Egypt, but in Europe there was a lull following the decline of the Roman Empire. However, through the 13th century, European glassmaking gathered pace, with Venice emerging as the center for decorative glass and northern Europe pioneering an industry producing glass for windows.

Initially, window glass was formed from blown glass cylinders, which were split and flattened while still hot. The sections of glass produced were small with irregular clarity, but could be incorporated together with the use of lead wire to fill large openings for windows. Crown glass, a French development, appeared in 1330. This was blown glass spun to form a disk and then trimmed into square panes, characterized by a round, central dimple. The glass produced was reasonably clear and widely used in windows up to the mid-19th century.

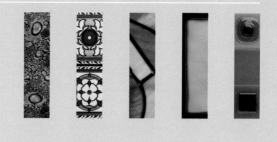

Glass size, flatness and clarity were gradually improved through a combination of hand and mechanical polishing and grinding, but it was not until the beginning of the 20th century that technology was able to develop beyond hand-blown techniques to machine-manufactured glass. The size of the cylinder of glass used to form flat panes gradually increased, reducing textural imperfections.

Eventually it became possible to form flat glass that could be cut when cooled. Float glass, which is the basis for today's modern glass, was developed only in 1959. This is formed by floating molten glass on top of molten tin in a frame. New glass is being developed all the time, with increased size, structural abilities or surface strength, large or small curves, UV filters and solar reflectors, smart glass, which can change from clear to opaque at a touch, and self-cleaning glass.

When planning to use glass, it is important that safety is considered. All glass intended for installation at low levels should be reinforced and all structural glass will require calculations to confirm its integrity for authority inspectors. It is also worth considering when planning a project that, not only do you risk the fishbowl effect of living in a glass structure, but also be aware of the lantern effect, as your glass will augment the amount of light released upon your neighbors and the night sky.

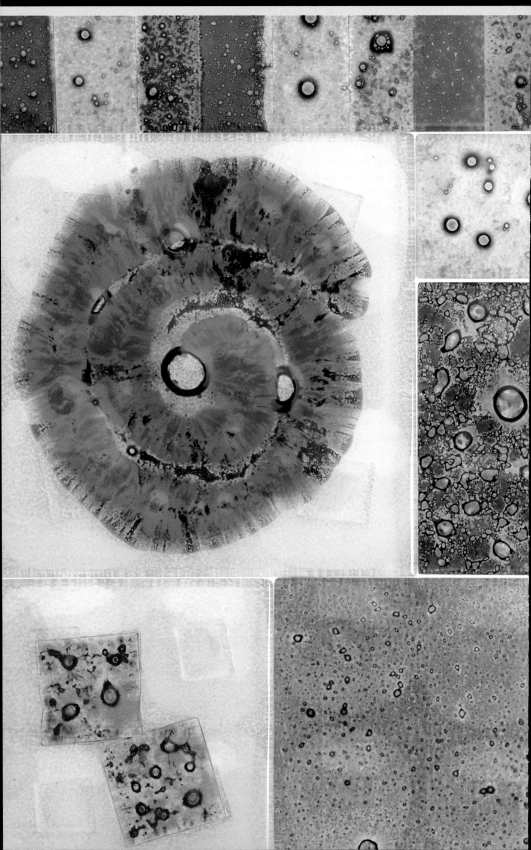

LAMINATED AND LAYERED GLASS

Laminating glass, either by adhering two or more layers together or by coating a layer of glass with a clear plastic film, has a number of performance and decorative advantages. It strengthens glass without reducing its appearance and opens up the opportunity to "capture" different effects between the layers. Laminates are suitable for use indoors or out, as a decorative or a structural component.

Properties: Glass itself is not affected by light or water, or subject to staining or heat damage, but grit exposure causes wear (as on sea glass). All glass becomes increasingly brittle at very low temperatures. Film-laminated sheets of glass have increased impact resistance: one example is bulletproof glass. Sheets can also be laminated with reflective film to deflect sunlight and reduce solar gain — the buildup of heat from the sun shining through glass. A glass surface is generally smooth, strong, scratch-resistant and hygienic, although it can be textured. Glass can be completely transparent or just translucent.

Use and Maintenance: Laminated glass can be used as a structural material for sunrooms, countertops, stair treads, tabletops and supports. It is a required safety feature in many situations, such as full-length glass doors or large screens. Decorative intermediate layers, sandwiched between protective layers of glass, might include woven fabric, objects such as pressed flowers, metal, colored film or even glass fragments, producing an effect that looks like broken glass, but is safe and easy to care for. Such decorative laminated panels can be used as screens, partitions and balustrading, or in garden installations and water features. Sheets can be treated with additional processes — etched, sandblasted, colored, curved — for different effects. Laminates are hard-wearing and easy to clean with glass cleaner or vinegar.

Safety and Environment: Glass is a long-lasting, stable material that can be recycled.

Availability: Glass that is laminated for performance reasons — i.e., for structural strength, fire tolerance or solar reflection — is readily available, although sheets will have to be cut to order. Most decorative laminates are made to order (to your requirements) from an architectural glass supplier.

Cost: ❹ High.

Specifications: Standard clear glass comes in 8 thicknesses (⅛–1 in/4–25 mm); tinted glass in fewer. Size and location of holes for fixtures must be drilled by the manufacturer and agreed upon when ordering.

ETCHED AND SANDBLASTED GLASS

Sandblasting glass or etching it with acid creates a frosted pattern and gives sheet glass a subtle three-dimensional texture. These effects can be used to give a flat translucence to windows, to increase security or privacy (in bathrooms, for instance), or as decoration; etched patterns or script are often seen on glazed front doors or on fanlight windows above entrances.

Properties: Etching is formed by "bite and grind": after masking off areas of pattern that are not to be etched, the glass is painted with bitumen-based paint, then "bitten" into with an acid wash and ground with fine sand. Sandblasting creates various tones, depths and textures by blasting different sizes of grit at the glass through compressed air. Patterns appear whitish and cloudy, whether on clear or colored glass, and are equally translucent from both sides. They also have a matte texture that clears slightly when wet. The surface of the untreated side is usually smooth. Glass worked in this way maintains all the properties of untreated glass.

Use and Maintenance: Decorative visual effects can range from random texturing (for repetitive, geometric or spontaneous patterns) to figurative designs or text (for signage). When intended to increase privacy, the treated surface should be fitted facing inside, as rain on the etched side increases transparency. Etching can also reduce solar gain by limiting direct sunlight. Patterning is also used for safety, for example on large expanses of glass that might otherwise appear invisible, or to reduce the slipperiness of polished glass floors. Etching is also used decoratlvely on mirrors, lamps, tables and dividing screens. The acid-etched look can be simulated by adhesive transfer film.

Safety and Environment: This long-lasting, safe, stable material is recyclable.

Availability: Frosting and three-dimensional sandblasting feature in many glass products (vases, stemware, ornaments). Use glass suppliers and specialized processing firms to locate companies that etch to order; some prepatterned panes are stocked by door and window manufacturers. Etched-glass screens, mirrors and art objects turn up in salvage yards and antique stores.

Cost: ❸–❺ Medium to very high.

Specifications: Most projects must be specially made to your requirements. Effects can be negative format (frosted background and clear pattern) or positive format (clear background, frosted pattern).

WOOD • RUBBER, PLASTIC, RESIN & LINOLEUM • METAL • **GLASS** • FABRIC • PAPER • LEATHER • PAINT, VARNISH & LACQUER • STONE, CERAMICS & TILES • CONCRETE & CEMENT • PLASTER

STAINED AND LEADED GLASS

INTERIOR MATERIALS & SURFACES: THE COMPLETE GUIDE

STAINED AND LEADED GLASS

The technique of joining together small sections of colored glass with lead wire to create a pattern, scene or image has changed little over the centuries. It was originally favored by the Church (few others could afford it) for religious iconography to glorify God. Art Nouveau designers such as Louis Comfort Tiffany brought to it a new elegance, and restorers and some modern artists keep the craft alive.

Properties: Most examples are handmade, so quality depends on the maker's technical and artistic skills. Glass is stained by mixing pigment with molten glass; colors are either uniformly mixed or graduated. Pieces can also be hand-painted, acid-etched or sandblasted. Geometric or irregular shapes are joined together with lead or copper, soldered at each joint and attached using lead light cement. The lead and cement are susceptible to atmospheric degeneration and if unprotected will require careful maintenance and, possibly, resetting (after about 15 years). Pigments alter the glass's properties; most cause weakening. Stained-glass panes are as strong as their leaded connections, but some newer installations are laminated for extra security.

Use and Maintenance: Stained glass in windows can be used decoratively, as a visual security screen (in place of drapes or blinds) or to diffuse sunlight. It requires careful maintenance and works best if illuminated by natural light or lamplight. It is

not structurally secure without backing glass. Common uses are windows, screens, doors and decorative objects. Leaded windows often feature beveled glass (with angled perimeters) to enhance the three-dimensional effect. New stained glass, leaded or beveled windows can be produced to suit double-glazed windows. A leaded look can be achieved with liquid lead, a product applied to the insides of windows.

Safety and Environment: Old stained glass is usually salvaged and reused rather than recycled.

Availability: Individual artisans will take on many types of projects to suit specific requirements. Larger stained-glass manufacturers will usually take on small one-off projects, as well as commercial commissions. Raw materials are available from artists' suppliers, colored glass from glass suppliers.

Cost: ❹ High.

Specifications: There are around 200 colors of stained glass available.

WOOD • RUBBER, PLASTIC, RESIN & LINOLEUM • METAL • **GLASS** • FABRIC • PAPER • LEATHER • PAINT, VARNISH & LACQUER • STONE, CERAMICS & TILES • CONCRETE & CEMENT • PLASTER

INTERIOR MATERIALS & SURFACES: THE COMPLETE GUIDE

GLASS BLOCKS

GLASS BLOCKS

Glass blocks, which can be solid or hollow, are made of thick glass in a variety of sizes and surface textures. They can be used singly, or stacked to create partitions or screens. The blocks allow light through but distort the view, and can create stunning effects when they are imaginatively illuminated by natural or feature lighting.

Properties: Glass blocks are strong in compression, but must be nonload-bearing and isolated from the surrounding structure with an expansion joint. Long walls require supporting where there is no lateral stability. Make allowance for extra weight on the existing structure — glass blocks are very heavy. Blocks are grouted together and the grout silicone-sealed. The block's thickness and/or hollow center distorts light, reducing transmission to 75 percent, so close-up objects appear shadowy and those farther away become invisible. A block's air pocket also provides some acoustic insulation. Blocks do not encourage fire spread; most new blocks have a minimum fire rating of 45 minutes.

Use and Maintenance: Use blocks for external cladding, for panels where light without visibility is desirable or for areas prone to vandalism (such as basement windows). They are particularly effective as internal walls to allow, for example, borrowed light into a hallway. They perform well in showers and bathrooms as partitions or exterior walls. Walls can be curved, to a minimum inner radius of 31½ inches or 8 feet (80 cm or 2.5 meters), depending on block size. Successful glass block features include precast stair treads, kitchen screens and translucent room dividers. Blocks can be inset into floors or walkways to relieve solid textures or allow light through. They are also used for built-in, outdoor furniture or water features.

Safety and Environment: Glass is long-lasting, so it can be reused. Damaged blocks can be recycled.

Availability: From glass suppliers, building centers and home-improvement retailers. Specially formulated grout sold with the product. As blocks are easily reclaimed, they can also be sourced from architectural salvage companies. Types are: solid, patterned or treated (for fire rating).

Cost: ❸ Medium.

Specifications: Standard blocks: 4 x 8 in (10 x 20 cm), 6 x 6 in (15 x 15 cm), 8 x 8 in (20 x 20 cm), 1 x 1 ft (30 x 30 cm). Curved blocks available (allowing internal radius of 1 ft/30 cm).

WOOD • RUBBER, PLASTIC, RESIN & LINOLEUM • METAL • **GLASS** • FABRIC • PAPER • LEATHER • PAINT, VARNISH & LACQUER • STONE, CERAMICS & TILES • CONCRETE & CEMENT • PLASTER

SLUMPED GLASS

INTERIOR MATERIALS & SURFACES: THE COMPLETE GUIDE

SLUMPED GLASS

Slumping creates glass objects by heating glass in a kiln to a temperature where it softens enough to "slump" into the shape of a mold. This process is often used together with fusing to mix glass of different colors. It is an old craft technique that is used by glass-processing companies to produce effects for a variety of decorative purposes.

Properties: A sheet of glass is placed on a heat-resistant mold (ceramic or steel) and heated in a kiln to approximately 1200°F (650°C), causing the glass to soften and fall into the mold. The molded pattern often varies in depth and features tiny bubbles that diffuse light and distort images, reducing visibility but creating a dramatic effect. Different colors can be used and fused together at a slightly higher temperature. It is important that any glasses used have the same properties. Slumped glass possesses identical properties to sheet glass (see Laminated and Layered Glass, page 91).

Use and Maintenance: Slumped-glass forms are used sculpturally for their decorative appeal or functionally to increase privacy while retaining light. In architectural design, slumped glass can be used for furniture, doors, windows, dividing walls and kitchen or bathroom surfaces. It makes attractive bathroom screens, shower surrounds and basin bowls. Slumped and fused glass is now also formed into modules that work with ceramic tiles as feature insets (see page 205). They must be applied with special adhesives and, being transparent, care should be taken with any colors underneath. Slumped glass is used decoratively in craftwork too, for bowls and for other containers. Use glass cleaners, but protect textured areas from soiling as dried-on deposits are difficult to remove.

Safety and Environment: Slumped glass products, particularly crafts, often use recycled glass.

Availability: As a high level of prefabrication will be required, slumped glass will have to be sourced directly from a manufacturer. You can find contact details for manufacturers through building centers.

Cost: ❹ High.

Specifications: Some patterns commercially available, but most projects are one-off commissions. Items up to about 9 ft (2.7 m) square and 1 in (2.5 cm) thick can be created, with patterns or textures.

FABRIC

The technique of weaving originated in Mesopotamia in 5000 BCE, where flax was harvested and woven to make linen. Linen was used for making early clothing, some of which survives in the funeral shrouds of the pharaohs. By 2500 BCE the Egyptians were cultivating cotton and weaving it into cloth. In other parts of the world, as animals were domesticated in the late Stone Age, the predominant source of early yarn was wool, shorn from sheep and processed into garments, blankets and sacking. China, meanwhile, had developed silk in about 2600 BCE. The secret of this cloth was carefully guarded for around 3,000 years before eventually spreading to Japan and India.

Although the processing and dyeing of the raw materials can create a variety of textured fibers, cloth is almost entirely manufactured by either weaving or knitting the threads or yarn together. Combinations of more than one fiber, for example silk and cotton or wool and linen, can alter the properties of the cloth to create, for instance, a fine, smooth, diaphanous fabric, a bulky material that will absorb sound or a strong, stiff fabric that will maintain its intended shape.

It was not until the 20th century that man-made fibers emerged. Rayon, which was produced from wood or cotton pulp in the United States in 1910, was the first. It was known as artificial silk, but was soon replaced by fabric that was produced from

petrochemical processing rather than from natural materials. Nylon, introduced in 1939, was the first completely new synthetic fiber — made using new technology and newly discovered synthetic materials. Other synthetic fibers, such as acetate, acrylic, polyester, triacetate, spandex and polyolefin were developed during the 1950s and 1960s. In the 1980s and 1990s increasingly sophisticated technology led to the development of microfibers from many synthetic fibers, and lyocell, an environmentally friendly fiber produced from wood pulp.

Each synthetic fiber has been created to replace a rarely available or expensive natural product and to exhibit particular qualities. For instance, fibers such as Kevlar, as used in bulletproof vests, have been developed to be stronger than steel, while Gore-Tex was pioneered as a breathable fabric that is both wind- and water-resistant.

In the home, it is now possible to take advantage of many fabrics' specific qualities, from resistance to fading, wrinkling and staining to washability or increased acoustic effects, and most fabrics are labeled with recommendations for uses and methods of cleaning. Fabrics can be specially treated to withstand staining or to limit the spread of fire, and it is advisable that all flammable fabrics intended for upholstery, drapery or decorating be treated for fire resistance (this is a legal requirement in some countries).

COTTON

 Woven cotton's wide range of strengths, thicknesses and textures, and its adaptability to numerous color and surface treatments, make it probably the most widely used natural fabric. It is invaluable in the production of clothing and in industry as well as most home furnishings, from luxurious fine-weave drapes to tough canvas; highly decorative designs to utilitarian ticking and calico undercovers for upholstery.

Properties: Cotton grows in the southern United States, Asia and Africa. The thread is spun from the fluffy, durable fibers that form around the plant's seed. The woven cloth can be dense or loose, rough or smooth. It is strong along and across the grain, but distorts on the diagonal. It can be dyed industrially or by hand. It is mixed with other fibers, both natural and man-made ("cotton rich" fabric must contain 60 percent or more cotton). Cotton is naturally hydrophilic, attracting and absorbing water readily, but will mildew if left damp. Strong acids (e.g., sulfuric) and oxidizing agents (e.g., chlorine bleach) cause deterioration. Cotton is combustible, but can be fireproofed with chemical treatment.

Use and Maintenance: Cotton is a cost-effective, durable fabric for home furnishings. Choose weaves and weights recommended for the intended purpose: lighter weights are suitable for cushion covers, light drapes and bed linen (cotton may help ease the discomfort of skin conditions such as eczema).

Canvas is popular for outdoor use, for canopies, awnings and seat covers. Certain cloths, such as inexpensive calico, come in extra-wide rolls ideal for draperies or opulent effects. Scraps and offcuts are also utilized for crafts such as patchwork. Clean cotton with fabric cleaners, or in line with color or pattern requirements. Dry without delay.

Safety and Environment: Cotton in the home can reduce levels of chemicals released from cleaning products, paints, varnishes and foam. Cotton is also biodegradable and breaks down completely in landfill sites.

Availability: From fabric stores, department and home-improvement stores, artists' suppliers and specialized suppliers. Upholstery cotton can also be sourced from furniture stores. Also available ready-made into soft furnishings and accessories.

Cost: ❶–❸ Very low to medium.

Specifications: Sold by length in various widths: most common are 48, 54 and 60 in (122, 137 and 150 cm); some up to 5.5 yd (5 m) wide. (See also Carpets and Rugs, page 117.)

WOOL

Woolen fabrics are woven from the fibers collected from the coats of fleecy animals — most often sheep, but also other animals such as goats and llamas. Wools have a variety of textures, from coarse, rough homespuns or tweeds to smooth, fine cloths that are extremely soft and warm to the touch. Wool fabrics are generally produced for upholstery, clothing, blankets and insulation.

Properties: After shearing, the fleece from sheep is graded, carded and spun into yarn. The fibers' natural crimp, or curl, creates pockets of air, giving wool a soft, spongy feel, high sound absorbency and low thermal conductivity (which reduces heat loss). Wool takes and keeps color exceptionally well. Fabrics have fuzzy surfaces, natural bulk and resilience, and do not hold creases (worsted woolens are processed to enable pressing). Due to its high moisture and nitrogen content, wool is the most naturally flame-retardant fiber, and highly hydrophilic — it absorbs up to 30 percent of its weight in moisture (and desorbs without damaging the fabric). Wool can neutralize many acids and it also absorbs chemical contaminants released in the home.

Use and Maintenance: The soft texture of wool is ideal for upholstery, but choose heavy-duty upholstery grades in areas of high wear. Clothing-weight wools can be used for cushions, screens and drapes. Wool carpets are high quality, long-lasting and easy maintenance, with strong, true colors. Wools often feature in handmade artifacts, such as blankets and throws. They are easy maintenance, resisting soiling and repelling surface spills. Vacuum carpets and upholstery regularly. Clean with fabric cleaners or as per color or pattern requirements, and dry without delay. (See also Carpets and Rugs, page 117, and Felt Fabric, page 125.)

Safety and Environment: Wool is a naturally grown, renewable resource that is recyclable and biodegradable. However, some species, such as the llama's relative the vicuña, are killed for their coats, so conservation measures are necessary.

Availability: Easily sourced in fabric stores. Specialty wools (usually plucked rather than shorn) from angora rabbit, cashmere goat, camel and alpaca come from specialized suppliers or breeders.

Cost: ❸–❹ Medium to high.

Specifications: Sold by length in various widths: most common are 48, 54 and 60 in (122, 137 and 150 cm). (See also Carpets and Rugs, page 117.)

MAN-MADE FABRICS

While cloths from natural fibers have their own varying personalities, man-made fibers have been developed to be woven into fabrics with specific characteristics. These synthetic fabrics may possess particularly sophisticated qualities — weatherproofing or resistance to creasing, for example — or mimic the look of costly natural fabrics without the expense. Many fabrics are made from a mix of natural and synthetic fibers.

Properties: Man-made fibers are produced by extruding filaments from a chemical mix in liquid form. Colors are usually added at the liquid stage and synthetics do not often hold dyes well after this. There are numerous man-made fabrics, each with its own properties. Examples include spandex (with increased elasticity), nylon (lightweight, weatherproof, durable) and rayon (soft and silky). Man-made fibers can change the properties of natural fibers: polyester woven with cotton provides a noncrease ("perma-press") quality. They can also contain integral fire retardant. Some new man-made fabrics have high-performance levels initially, but these can often reduce after numerous washes. Many man-mades are vulnerable if subject to solvents or to high temperatures, melting under a hot iron.

Use and Maintenance: Man-made fabrics can be used decoratively, for cushion covers, screens and drapes, in the same way as similar natural fabrics. They can be resistant to sunlight and moisture damage, so are ideal outdoors and as sunshades. They can provide many different effects: a silklike material that is not fragile or prohibitively expensive, for instance, or realistic faux furs (see also page 123). Those containing spandex or elastane can be stretched over wire frames to form storage boxes or light fixtures (the latter must be fireproof). Use fabric cleaners or clean as per color/pattern requirements.

Safety and Environment: Man-made fabrics are often formed through processes that use toxic chemicals, and are not always biodegradable. Some have a valid environmental use in replacing products acquired from endangered species.

Availability: Wide range of synthetic fabrics, for domestic or industrial use, from fabric stores. Also available ready-made into soft furnishings and accessories.

Cost: ❷–❸ Low to medium.

Specifications: Sold by length in various widths: most common are 48, 54 and 60 in, (122, 137 and 150 cm), but also in narrower and wider measures. (See also Carpets and Rugs, page 117.)

KNITTED FABRICS

Unlike the simple warp and weft of woven fabrics, knitted fabrics such as jersey are formed by interlacing a series of looping threads or yarns using needles or wires — essentially the same process as knitting wool into sweaters or scarves. This method gives knits a varying degree of elasticity, and knitted materials have a slightly deeper pile than a woven fabric of the same yarn.

Properties: Different knitting techniques produce various textures. Different yarns, both man-made and natural, can be used within each knit and will retain their properties. Knits will not fray, but may unravel. Many are prone to wear and tear and have a tendency to "pill," developing small balls of fibers on the surface. Due to the tiny air pockets trapped by the knitting process, knits have a high level of thermal insulation. They also possess acoustic-insulation properties, although a very loose knit will have most value in absorbing or deadening sound when placed against a solid surface. They are easy to treat with fire retardant.

Use and Maintenance: Thinner knitted fabrics, such as jersey, can be draped or stretched to form infill panels for storage unit doors or to cover frames to act as light diffusers. Thicker knitted fabrics have increased heat retention, making them useful for blankets, throws and accessories such as cushions. They make attractive wall hangings, creating a feeling of warmth and coziness. Knits should not be used in areas of heavy wear or will pill (it is possible to remove pills by trimming them with a razor). Cleaning is dependent on which fibers are used in their manufacture, but all knits are susceptible to damage by dust, so they require regular vacuuming, emergency spot-cleaning and dry-cleaning or laundering at intervals.

Safety and Environment: Knits are safe to produce, but are made from various fibers, some naturally grown and biodegradable, others synthetic; synthetic fibers may not break down.

Availability: Drapery fabrics from fabric stores and specialized suppliers. Upholstery can also be sourced from furniture stores. Knits intended for clothing (but suitable for craft or art use) from fabric and specialty stores.

Cost: ❷–❸ Low to medium.

Specifications: Upholstery or curtain fabric sold by length in the same variable widths as woven fabrics.

GAUZES

Gauze is a very thin, transparent fabric that is made from a loose, open weave. The light, floaty style that this material gives summer dresses has inspired designers to use it in the home in a number of ways. Gauzes are often made from fine fibers such as silk or cotton, but they are also available woven from thin plastic threads and fine-gauge metal strands.

Properties: Silk gauze is lightweight and sheer, giving a translucent effect that allows visibility into the side with greater light. Most gauzes are delicate and easily torn, and floppy rather than stiff — except metal gauzes, which can be folded. Weave densities and patterns vary from the extremely even, fine vision gauze to the distinctly rectangular net effect of sharkstooth (larger-weave fabrics are called netting). Gauzes are easily stretched and distorted on the bias — a loose weave means this is often permanent. Some gauzes are treated with fire retardant.

Use and Maintenance: Most gauzes are very delicate, so they are best used for decoration. They can be held taut, gathered, folded or creased, used alone or as an overlay, allowing another fabric underneath to show through. They work well gathered, providing an opulent effect without bulk, for cascading behind decorative drapes or for tenting over a bed. They can be stretched over a frame to make screens and wall hangings. Cotton gauze (as used in bandaging) is used to give structure to plaster and clay in craftwork. Metal gauzes have industrial applications as filters, but they may feature as decorative and sculptural elements in the home. Silk and cotton gauzes can be washed on a delicate machine cycle; other fibers may have special care instructions. Use fabric cleaners or follow color/pattern requirements. Dry without delay.

Safety and Environment: Environmental rating is dependent on the nature of its fibers: natural fibers break down or can be recycled; synthetics will not usually biodegrade, but some can be recycled.

Availability: A varied range available for domestic or craft use from fabric stores, artists' suppliers and specialty stores.

Cost: ❷–❸ Low to medium.

Specifications: Sold by length in various widths: most common are 48, 54 and 60 in (122, 137 and 150 cm). Also as ready-made draperies and accessories such as lampshades.

SILK

Silk is one of the oldest textile fabrics, treasured for its strength and beauty. It has been used by the Chinese since 2700 BCE and was a valued commodity in ancient Greece and the Roman Empire. Silk thread is obtained by unwinding the strands cocooning the pupae (silkworms) of several moth species. Silk fabrics are elegant and versatile, and always associated with wealth and luxury.

Properties: Its fine, lightweight appearance is deceptive: silk is the strongest fiber, stronger than an equally sized steel thread. Silk has a lustrous, shimmering appearance and drapes beautifully. Traditional, glossy cloth is called China silk, but silk fabrics include soft, transparent georgettes, chiffons and organzas; dupion, which is woven from short and long fibers for a slightly ribbed, "slubbed" effect; and velvets and corduroys with a soft pile. Silk's high absorbency allows it to take deep, vibrant dyes, but also means fluids such as oil, wax and petroleum are difficult to remove. Sunlight causes deterioration.

Use and Maintenance: Dupion is popular for feature upholstery and drapery because of its luxurious feel and deep colors. It is lightweight and gathers beautifully, but drapes need lining to protect against fading and damage from the sun. It can be ruched for tented ceilings, canopies and wallcoverings. Chiffon and organza make attractive screens, cushions and lampshades, but they will deteriorate in sunlight so are not suitable over windows. Silk also makes very soft carpets and rugs (see page 117). Avoid using in kitchens or areas containing grease or oil. All silk is hand- or machine-washable on a delicate cycle. It does not shrink but will wrinkle, so some items should be sponged or dry-cleaned. Silk dries quickly and can be damaged by heat, so do not machine dry.

Safety and Environment: Silk is produced naturally and biodegrades quickly in sunlight.

Availability: Wide range from fabric stores, artists' suppliers and specialized suppliers. Silk upholstery fabric is also available from furniture stores. Also sold as ready-made draperies and accessories such as cushions and lampshades.

Cost: ❹ High.

Specifications: By length in various widths: most common are 36, 48 and 54 in (90, 122 and 137 cm), although other widths are available.

TRIBAL PRINTED CLOTH

African printed cloth (*kitenge*) is cotton painted with brightly colored graphic patterns and used to make garments. Although distinctly African in design and use, many fabrics are produced in India or Europe and exported to West and East Africa, the Middle East, Singapore and Spain (some handmade prints are produced in The Gambia). Patterns are colorful and dynamic, representing local culture and traditions.

Properties: Almost all *kitenge* is 100 percent cotton. Many patterns are created with a mechanically applied wax-resist that imitates handmade Indonesian batik. Most designs have a natural theme, such as animals, birds or flowers, but subjects are limitless. In Mali, traditional *kolokane* or mud cloth is made by stitching together strips or panels of handwoven or spun cloth, then painting them (usually with cultural symbols) using aged river mud containing iron oxides and other earth pigments. Fabrics are usually stiff when purchased, but soften after washing. Cloths are made of rugged, durable fibers that naturally attract and absorb water, and will mildew if left damp. They are unaffected by organic solvents, but strong acids and chlorine bleach cause deterioration. Fabrics are naturally combustible, but can be chemically fireproofed.

Use and Maintenance: Because prints appear on both sides, fabrics can be gathered, twisted and draped without the need for lining. Use wherever cotton is appropriate: patchwork quilting, upholstery, cushion covers, drapes, wall hangings and throws. Colors are durable, as they are made to withstand vigorous hand washing, but dark shades should be washed separately initially to remove any excess dyes. These tribal-print fabrics are machine-washable, but any applied stain- or fire-resistant products will be removed in the wash.

Safety and Environment: The use of natural cotton in the home can reduce levels of contaminants. These fabrics are biodegradable, breaking down completely in landfill sites.

Availability: A few available from fabric stores, but most available from specialty fabric stores in areas within African communities or at local African markets. Sometimes available ready-made as cushions or quilts.

Cost: ❷ Low.

Specifications: Sold by length, 44 in (112 cm) wide. Rolls are 17½ or 35 ft (5.4 or 10.8 m) long. Sold in Africa in rolls or in 6½ ft (2 m) lengths. *Kolokane*: 45 x 36 or 72 in (120 x 90 or 180 cm).

CARPETS AND RUGS

Ranging from broadloom fitted for an entire room to stair runners and feature rugs, carpets bring a sense of warmth and softness to a room. As well as their practical advantages, they can generate visual interest, and their use need not be limited to covering the floor. The choice of designs, textures and fibers is huge, but there is usually a direct correlation between cost and performance.

Properties: Wool is the most common fiber in carpets and rugs, but cotton, silk, linen and synthetics are also often found, either alone or in combination. Carpeting is categorized by style of pile. Broadloom is commonly twist pile (fibers gathered together, twisted and trimmed); velvet pile (more luxurious in appearance); or loop pile (left uncut for a nubbed look). Cut piles display a nap when brushed. Also available are flat-weaves, typical of traditional handmade rugs. Denser piles are more durable and retain their looks for longer. Hand-knotted rugs often use high-quality wool or silk and are long-lasting. New carpeting is fire-treated; check that antique and imported rugs are too. Many natural rugs are not moth-resistant.

Use and Maintenance: Choose a fiber composition suitable for the location. Most handmade carpets are quality wools, but synthetics in the mix reduce cost and can introduce specific qualities. Good underlay can improve durability and appearance by 40 percent. Leather-soled shoes "polish" carpets, but rubber soles can quickly destroy them. Rugs can be functional, to protect flooring or muffle footsteps, or be a decorative feature. On walls they give a warm, rich effect, and can reduce noise levels and increase insulation. Grit is the main culprit in carpet wear; vacuum regularly, and vacuum rugs from top and bottom. Shampoo periodically and remove stains with proprietary cleaner.

Safety and Environment: Carpet manufacturers are generally part of a best-practice program, monitoring ethical production and recycling of waste.

Availability: From carpet or flooring stores and department stores; antique carpets and rugs from dealers and antique outlets. Broadloom sold by area; runners by length.

Cost: ❸–❹ Medium to high; price and quality depend on fibers, weaving type and backing (rubber or hessian).

Specifications: Cut to any size within available widths of 6½ or 13 ft (2 or 4 m). Can be edge-bound with cloth tape for rugs and runners.

SEAGRASS, JUTE, SISAL AND COIR

Floorcoverings made from grasses and plant fibers such as seagrass, jute, sisal and coir are known as natural fiber carpets. Their use has increased over the last 15 years as they have come to be appreciated as an alternative to wool or synthetic carpets, where a natural or rustic look, but something softer and quieter than natural wood floors, is desired.

Properties: Seagrass is woven into tough, slightly shiny, reasonably stain-resistant matting. Jute is one of the softer, less durable plant fibers and prone to staining. Sisal, from the spiky sisal bush, has a fairly soft texture, but is extremely hard-wearing. These are usually woven rather than tufted, and require a thick, stable backing (usually supplied) to retain their loose weave. Coir, formed from coconut husks into a short, rough pile, is fairly tough and resists moisture, but the fibers may break with heavy use. These natural fibers have a detectable aroma. Stain resistance for all these materials is generally poor, so color and pattern should be selected for practicality; all except coir will mildew if left damp.

Use and Maintenance: Natural fiber carpets feature geometric and herringbone patterns, and do not show wear. They are unsuitable for kitchens or dining rooms (where they may be stained), or for stairs, where their natural shine may be polished and become slippery. Coir makes excellent entrance matting; its bristles help to remove grit from footwear. All natural fiber carpets have a deep texture and so will need frequent vacuuming to prevent dust and grit from dulling their appearance. Protect from bright sunlight to prevent color fading over time. Jute is effective as an underlay for rugs prone to "walking" across the floor, or used where soiling/staining is unlikely.

Safety and Environment: These materials are a nontoxic, natural industry product from developing countries. They are biodegradable, although any synthetic backing products should be removed separately.

Availability: From carpet suppliers, flooring suppliers, department stores and various home-improvement retailers.

Cost: ❹ High.

Specifications: Cut to any size within available widths of 6½ or 13 ft (2 or 4 m). Can be edge-bound with cloth tape for rugs and runners.

WOOD • RUBBER, PLASTIC, RESIN & LINOLEUM   METAL • GLASS • **FABRIC** • PAPER • LEATHER • PAINT, VARNISH & LACQUER   STONE, CERAMICS & TILES • CONCRETE & CEMENT   PLASTER

FLEECE

INTERIOR MATERIALS & SURFACES: THE COMPLETE GUIDE

FLEECE

Fleece generally refers to sheared sheep coats, which provide a thick, soft, organic product that is soft to the touch and possesses great natural warmth. Fleeces have a number of different characteristics depending on their source and the time of year they were cut. Fleece can also describe new, high-performance fabrics that are produced from synthetic materials and can mimic the properties of natural fleece.

Properties: Sheep are shorn in early autumn to allow a new coat to grow before winter, and in spring for a clean, even summer coat. Fleeces divide into the inner, downy "thel" and outer, coarser "tog." Thel is mixed with fine fibers (such as angora or silk) for specialist delicate blends. Tog is spun into yarn. Winter fleece is used for felting (see page 125). Wool holds dyes well and absorbs and desorbs water readily. It has a detectable aroma when wet and will mildew if left damp. Its moisture and nitrogen content make it naturally flame-retardant, and as an insulation material it is effective for reducing heat loss. Synthetic fleeces vary in weight and quality.

Use and Maintenance: Fleece is processed in numerous ways, creating warm products soft to the touch. Attached to a natural or synthetic backing, fleece is used for cushion covers and hearth rugs, and makes a safe and comforting liner for baby seats or strollers; it is also available on its original leather (see page 157). Fleece absorbs sound and generates a cozy atmosphere when used as wall hangings or throws. Fleece felting as carpet underlay is warm, durable and deadens sound. Synthetic acoustic underlay fleeces are also available. Dry-clean natural fleece products, or hand wash cold or machine wash cold on the delicate cycle. Protect exposed fibers from dust and vacuum regularly.

Safety and Environment: The use of natural fleece can reduce levels of chemical contaminants released in the home. Natural fleece is biodegradable, breaking down completely in landfill sites; synthetic fleece can be recycled.

Availability: Fabrics available from fabric stores, and artists' or specialized suppliers; insulating or acoustic fleeces from specialized building suppliers; carpet felt underlay from carpet or flooring suppliers.

Cost: ❸ Medium.

Specifications: Variable according to form: fabrics sold by length; insulation by volume. Also available as complete fleeces or offcuts, raw or dyed, for craft purposes.

FAUX FUR

Faux fur fabrics are manufactured with sophisticated synthetic fibers. They mimic real pelts from rare or endangered animals, and provide imitations of expensive furs or adaptations of unworkable skins such as porcupine. Alternatively, they can create new furry and fun textures, intentionally fake and often in outrageous colors. Faux furs can be used for a luxurious or humorous effect in soft furnishings and interiors.

Properties: Faux fur fabrics are made from synthetic fibers (usually acrylic). Imitation pelt lines, replicating traditional sewn pelts, are created during manufacture by shearing grooves. Although faux furs often appear cozy, most do not have the natural components that provide thermal or acoustic insulation. They are not damaged by water, but will lose some of their fluffiness when washed, so air-dry, separating and fluffing fibers by hand. Most fakes, except for those that are manufactured as rugs, do not wear well; longer piles flatten and become matted. All types are fire-retardant, but will melt in contact with candle flames or sparks from a fire.

Use and Maintenance: Faux furs usually have a backing material, which, if fleece or suede, can provide thermal insulation. They are suitable for working on home sewing machines or cutting with a knife (most do not fray). Various faux fur and faux wool yarns are available for knitting. Furs can be used to trim or as decorative strips. If used as upholstery, longer styles will wear, becoming flat and "yarny" or dreadlocked. Shorter piles make attractive covers for beanbags, floor cubes and ottomans. Fake furs are perfect for accessories, including cushion covers, lampshades and wall hangings, or mounted on a frame as a wallcovering. They are also used for pet furniture. Hand-wash in cool water but dry-clean longer furs to preserve texture.

Safety and Environment: The use of these synthetic fibers reduces the trade in fur from endangered species. Faux furs cannot be recycled.

Availability: Fabrics available from fabric stores or specialized suppliers; trim also available. Covered furniture or accessories sold in furniture and department stores and gift stores.

Cost: ❸ Medium.

Specifications: Sold on the roll in standard fabric widths, as ribbonlike trims or as individual pieces (for craftwork). Furs can be solid color, patterned or frosted (with tips a contrasting color).

FELT FABRIC

Felts are produced by compacting a mat of fibers with moisture, heat and pressure, to create a dense sheet. They can be made from wool, fur, cotton or synthetic fibers, or a mixture. Heavy-duty household felt is useful for insulation, backing and underlay, while felt craft fabrics, which usually come ready-dyed in a range of plain colors, can be sewn, woven, glued or molded into shapes.

Properties: Wool for felt is gathered from the spring-sheared winter fleece. It is processed into felt by arranging fibers in layers of alternating directions, then fusing them together using hot, soapy water, pressure and rubbing. Felt is generally quite stiff and does not fray, so can be used without any hemming to edges or cuts. Wool felts possess the same thermal and acoustic properties of all wool products; synthetic fiber felts, although similar in appearance, lack these properties. Felts are not damaged by water, but wool felts have a slight odor when wet.

Use and Maintenance: Felt can be formed into any shape by molding, to make home accessories such as decorative bowls and containers. Being easy to cut and nonfraying, felt is perfect for many handicraft projects. It can be cut into strips and woven or twisted to make cushion covers, mats, throws and wall hangings. It can also be perforated to make screens, panels or lampshades, and is useful for covering pinboards because pins will not leave holes in felt. During manufacture, felt can be given a decorative cross-section by layering with different colored fibers; this effect then becomes visible along cut edges or perforations. Felting for carpet underlay is durable, warm and acoustic. When used as a wallcovering, felt has a soft, rustic feel and absorbs sound, but also smells.

Safety and Environment: Felt made from natural wools can reduce levels of contaminants released in the home. Natural materials are also biodegradable and break down in landfill sites. Synthetic fiber felts can be recycled.

Availability: From fabric stores, artists' suppliers and specialized suppliers. Upholstery felt can be sourced from furniture and department stores.

Cost: ❸ Medium.

Specifications: Ready-cut felt squares: 12 x 12 in (30 x 30 cm); rolls: 32 in (80 cm) wide and (usually) ½₂ in (2 mm) thick. Felt underlay: 6½ ft (2 m) wide and about ⅙ in (4 mm) thick.

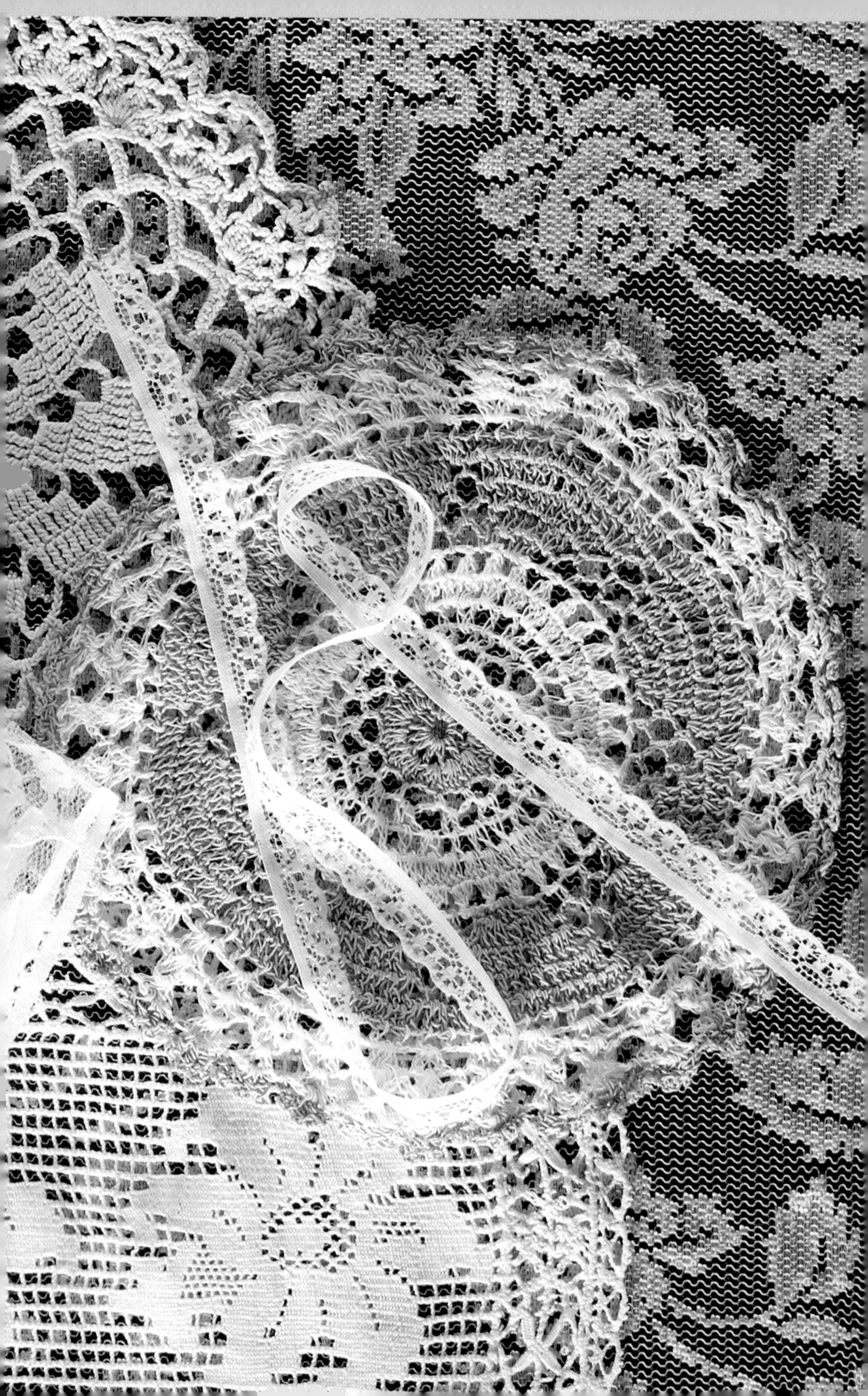

WOOD ● WOODEN, PLASTIC, RESIN & LINOLEUM ● METAL ● GLASS   FABRIC ● PAPER ● LEATHER   PAINT, VARNISH & LACQUER   STONE, SLATE ● & TILES   CONCRETE & CEMENT   [■■ ■ ■]

WOVEN NET

INTERIOR MATERIALS & SURFACES: THE COMPLETE GUIDE

WOVEN NET

The term "net" is used to describe many different fabrics, from large and small fishing nets to mosquito nets. Its varying degrees of translucence make it useful in a variety of ways, and fine net fabric, also known as tulle, is often used in creating an impression of bulk by layering under other fabrics — the ballet tutu has inspired similar creative applications in the home.

Properties: The intersections of a woven net are fused with pressure (or knotted, as for fishing nets), making a loose, meshlike surface that will not unravel. Woven nets are usually made of synthetic fibers, and can be stiff or flexible, lightweight or heavy, depending on the type and gauge of yarns. They can also be transparent or sheer. Sheer nets have a translucent effect, allowing visibility through to the side with greater light (so sheer drapes will allow views out during the day, while obscuring the view in, but this will reverse once dusk falls). Net for drapery can be a uniform plain weave, have an overall pattern or incorporate a straight or shaped border, providing a decorative hem. Woven net should be treated with fire retardant.

Use and Maintenance: Net manufactured for industrial applications can often be adapted for drapery or design projects. It can provide lightweight backing to a piece of handicraft and loose weaves make decorative diffusers for light fixtures. Ruched into a froth, fine net provides inexpensive frills in a little girl's bedroom. Lace drapes complement traditional decor. Net fabrics can be washed and pressed, but should also be kept dust-free by vacuuming. Dust or sunlight can cause graying; restore crispness with special whitening products.

Safety and Environment: Woven net made of synthetic fibers does not biodegrade well and should be recycled.

Availability: Net fabric is available from fabric stores or ready-made as drapes, tablecloths, etc., from department stores. Woven net for specific or industrial uses is available from specialized suppliers, such as camping or fishing stores. Synthetic nets are often cheaper than muslin or gauze.

Cost: ❶–❸ Very low to medium.

Specifications: Produced in different gauges as filters (for sun, water, etc.). Net fabrics available in usual widths (see page 103) and also to match standard window and pelmet drops.

WOOD • RUBBER, PLASTIC, RESIN & LINOLEUM • METAL • GLASS • **FABRIC** • PAPER • LEATHER • PAINT, VARNISH & LACQUER • STONE, CERAMICS & TILES • CONCRETE & CEMENT • PLASTER

WOVEN BANDS, RIBBONS AND BRAIDS

INTERIOR MATERIALS & SURFACES: THE COMPLETE GUIDE

WOVEN BANDS, RIBBONS AND BRAIDS

Decorative fabric ribbons and braids are woven from a variety of natural and synthetic fibers to create an almost infinite range of textures, colors and effects for use as trim. Alongside classic satins and corded trim are more unusual variations: cotton with jute creates a particularly rustic feel, and sisal and raffia with leather or beads a tribal look.

Properties: Acrylic, acetate, viscose and metallic (or mixed) fibers are most commonly used, because they provide a stable, intensely colored finish. Cotton and silk are used when natural variation in color and texture is desirable. Ribbons and braids are woven flat, have plain, linear or lateral patterns and smooth, fringed or scalloped edges. Polyester satin ribbons come in solid, brilliant colors. Ribbons can be sheer, velvet or grosgrain (with lateral ridges). Braids have decorative wrapped, twisted or rolled cords and trim. Ribbons are available edged with metallic thread overstitching and some contain wire so they can be bent into sculptural shapes. Trim is usually manufactured to comply with regulations limiting fire spread.

Use and Maintenance: Much trim is designed and manufactured specifically for upholstery or drapery — uses include covering seams in fabric sections or highlighting outlines. The very ornate patterns of some trim can be a feature in themselves, especially when decorating lampshades or cushion covers. Ribbons and braids can be used to edge wallcoverings or screens to conceal their pins. Ribbons are generally strong enough to gather in fabrics or bind edges, but should not be used structurally as they distort when pulled taut. Complex textures and mixes of fabric are difficult to clean. Remove dust by vacuuming regularly and take measures to avoid stains or oily marks.

Safety and Environment: Fabric trim made of synthetic fibers does not biodegrade well and the variety of fibers used in some trim makes them very difficult to recycle.

Availability: From fabric stores and specialized suppliers. Trim for upholstery and drapery is available from drapery makers.

Cost: ❹ High.

Specifications: Satin ribbons (c. 50 colors) and up to 1½ in (40 mm) wide. Velvet and grosgrain in many colors, but fewer widths. Other trim in hundreds of colors and designs. Sold by spool or length.

PRINTED FABRIC

Machine-printing patterns onto prewoven fabric has many advantages, especially for cost, while hand-printed fabrics allow complete individuality. An infinite selection of imagery can be printed onto fabric, from bold, bright florals to random geometrics or photographs. Printed patterns can be used to cost-effectively replicate opulent designs that are woven into more expensive fabrics.

Properties: Printed fabric is not limited by weave pattern or the size or type of threads used. Prints are produced on many natural or synthetic cloths, using sophisticated photographic reproduction and color jet printing. They are applied to one side only and, unless the fabric is thin or porous, do not transfer through (so printed fabrics always have a front and back). Printed fabrics are usually washable, since dyes contain durable fixatives. Their structural or draping qualities depend on the fibers used, although dyes can sometimes stiffen fabric. Materials incorporated into furnishings or drapes are fireproofed, but some craft fabrics, or those intended for clothing, may need treating.

Use and Maintenance: Preprinted fabrics have a fixed repeat, allowing patterns to be matched when joining widths (check that the pattern is printed exactly square with the fabric's weave, or pattern-matching may cause distortion). Some prints may feature a border along one or both sides. Manual printing can create unique prints or individual features that follow contours or panels (for instance, decorative borders on blinds, cushions or upholstery). There is a rising trend for hand-printed fabrics, often in muted colors, with irregular, elegant patterns. Printed fabrics are commonly used for upholstery, drapery, blinds, table and bed linen, lampshades and wall- and ceiling coverings. Most fixed dyes withstand whatever care is recommended for their base fabric.

Safety and Environment: Prints are often on cotton or natural fibers, which are safe and biodegradable. They can provide efficient added value to plain fabrics.

Availability: Wide range available from fabric stores, furnishers, upholsterers, specialized suppliers and directly from artists.

Cost: ❷–❹ Low to high depending on base material and print run.

Specifications: Almost all fabrics used in furniture, accessories or clothing have printed options.

PAPER

The word "paper" is derived from papyrus, which was developed by the ancient Egyptians, who manufactured it by hand from the pith of the papyrus reed growing along the Nile. Other cultures also developed paper-making techniques, using local plant materials such as the soft inner bark of mulberry, fig and daphne trees, indigenous to the Himalayas and south and eastern Asia. These various papers from different regions were generally known as tapa. Tapa was made by interlacing harvested plant fibers and hammering them to break up and fuse the fibers into a thin layer. These pulpy layers were soaked in water until they were soft and nearly transparent. They were then transferred to a netted mold so that the water could be pressed out. The resulting sheets of paper were simply hung up to dry in the sun. Handmade papers are still created using these traditional techniques.

Paper production was mechanized as early as 600 CE, when technology spread westward from China and paper mills were established in Baghdad and Damascus. Here the limited availability of natural fibers meant that rags were used as the main raw material. This technique evolved and spread into Europe. It was not until the mid-19th century that an alternative natural fiber was sought and ground softwood pulp replaced the use of rags.

Paper is a versatile material that can be used in numerous ways: scored, folded, curved, twisted, crumpled, cut or torn, treated with wax, glaze, enamel or metallicized. Paper can be opaque, translucent or transparent. It normally breaks down in water, but can be waterproofed; it is usually flammable, but can be made fire-resistant. It can be used alone or laminated to different papers or additional materials such as plastic film or wood, and can be a precious or disposable material.

Today paper has taken the place of many wood and cloth products, and paper products exist for specific applications around the home. As an essential building component, paper is used as a breather membrane in roofs and walls of lumber-framed buildings, and it provides a functional surface in the fabrication of drywall or as lining paper to cover new plaster, as a ground either for new paintwork or decorative wallpaper. As a finishing material, paper can be embossed, printed or flocked in sophisticated wallpaper patterns. Paper also provides the decorative layer of many high-pressure laminated sheets. Toughened or corrugated paper is used in construction to create forms for pouring concrete columns or making permanent or disposable furniture. At the other end of the scale, fragile or finely decorated handmade papers can embellish fixtures or home accessories.

TRADITIONAL HANDMADE PAPER

Various traditional handmade papers are manufactured today much as they were in ancient times. Papyrus, developed in ancient Egypt, is the best known handmade paper, but traditional papers are also still being made in the Far East and the Indian subcontinent from local plant fibers such as mulberry, banana and saa. Their individuality and texture make them attractive choices for various home projects.

Properties: Papyrus is made from the pith of the Nile's papyrus reed. Nepalese lokta paper is produced from Himalayan daphne bushes, while Japanese papers are made from indigenous gampi, mitsumata and kozo. Other fibers used include silk, cotton, linen and a sugarcane byproduct. After soaking in water, fibers are arranged in layers, pressed and beaten until the moisture is driven out and fibers fuse. A natural size, or glue, and decorative elements such as pigments or blossoms are sometimes added. Handmade papers have a rough, fibrous surface and deckled (slightly frayed) edges. They are durable, insect-resistant, absorbent yet strong even when soaked in water and acid-free (ideal for archival uses). Handmade papers are usually bleach-free, so will not yellow in sunlight.

Use and Maintenance: They make wonderful wallpaper, but long rolls are unavailable, so matching pieces over wide areas can be tricky. Papers can be block-printed, stenciled or painted.

Other uses are stationery, arts and crafts and bookmaking. Translucent kozo and mitsumata papers, traditionally used for *shoji* (screens) in Japan, work well as screens, blinds and lampshades. Acid-free paper is used in picture framing as mats (mounts) or to wrap framing sections. Stiff, heavier papers can make boxes and storage units.

Safety and Environment: These papers are made from cultivated bushes and reeds that regenerate yearly or, at most, within six years. They are gathered and processed ecologically and have a long life. Their production often supports local employment in areas of little economic activity and helps sustain ancient traditions.

Availability: Specialized paper importers/suppliers have a wide range; artists' suppliers offer a more limited selection.

Cost: ❶ High.

Specifications: Sheets are 18 x 18 in (450 x 450 mm) and 20 x 30 in (500 x 750 mm). Some papers may be limited or unique items, so check the amount you require is available when selecting.

EUROPEAN ART PAPER

The first European paper mill was built in Xativa, Spain, in 1009, by Arabs who learned the art from their Chinese prisoners. Today many decorative machined and handmade papers are produced for a variety of art, craft and finishing uses. Typically, these papers are either textured in the grain or by the inclusion of different materials, or have a highly decorative applied finish such as marbling or metallic effects.

Properties: Finishes and textures vary from the familiar wove (smooth) and laid (finely ridged) to fabriclike tweed, linen or silk; they may also be matte or glossy plastic-coated. Texture is known as "tooth," more tooth being desirable for drawing or painting, less for stamping or precise printing. Papers can be fused together so a sheet features a different color on the front and back. Many are acid-free, making them suitable next to fragile paper or fine art. Many art papers are delicate, thin and easy to tear, and some dyes, prints or stamps fade in sunlight.

Use and Maintenance: Various grades of paper and card featuring surreal or realistic marbled or metallic effects can be applied to household objects (for example, to cover shelves, tabletops or picture frames). Patterned or textured paper can provide an opulent effect when applied to door panels or walls (rolls for uniform wallpapering, however, are not available). Perforated sheets make decorative screens, blinds or lampshades. Stiff grades are used to make make small units or boxes — an alternative is to use a finer grade paper as a covering. Acid-free archival paper is used for picture mats (mounts) or to wrap framing sections. Other general uses include special stationery such as invitations, bookmaking and other arts and crafts.

Safety and Environment: Paper is produced from sustainable lumber stocks or domestically cultivated plants. Most gathering and processing is ecological, although some paints and glues are toxic. Most tree fiber papers biodegrade. All papers are fire hazards.

Availability: Specialized paper importers and suppliers have a broad range of art papers; limited selections are stocked by artists' suppliers.

Cost: ❹ High.

Specifications: Sheets approx 20 x 30 in (500 x 750 mm). Thousands of variations in fibers, textures, colors and effects are available. Some papers are limited or unique items, so check availability.

WRAPPING PAPER

Brown paper, printed wrapping papers and plastic foil are materials traditionally manufactured for packaging purposes. But they are versatile products that can be used in a variety of decorative or practical applications and arts and crafts projects — from lining drawers to stencil masks or reflective film for windows. The understated color of brown and pink craft paper is particularly popular.

Properties: Brown paper is smooth, with a visible woven texture. It can be pinkish, bleached or have a wax finish. Butcher paper (usually pink-tinged) is polyethylene-coated for durability — its primary use is for packaging frozen meat. Printed paper is more costly and decorative. It is either preprinted in mass production or custom-printed for personal use. All papers are porous and water-absorbent unless treated. Wrinkles caused by water damage are retained when dry. Wrapping papers are disposable and not strong. Plastic foil can have many metallic finishes, from slightly tinted transparent film to opaque silver. Foil is air- and watertight, strong in tension, but easily torn once pierced.

Use and Maintenance: Brown paper is economy paper used for utilitarian covering (when decorating) or a masking material for stencils (use waxed paper where moisture might buckle the paper). Other uses are as lining paper, to cover decorative screens, lampshades and even walls — it can be torn into pieces and glued in overlapped layers, much like papier-mâché, then varnished or painted. Untreated paper can be treated with size, or glue, to prevent moisture and oil absorption. A translucent silver variety of plastic foil, as used for bouquet wrapping and for packaging vacuum-packed foodstuffs, makes an effective reflective screen that allows light through while obscuring visibility.

Safety and Environment: Untreated papers are reasonably conscientiously produced and easily recycled. Plastic foil is only recycled by specialized companies who use it to make specific products.

Availability: Small sheets of wrapping paper or foil from stationery stores and artists' suppliers. Larger sheets and paper rolls can be ordered from packaging manufacturers. Large rolls of plastic foil can be ordered from plastic manufacturers.

Cost: ❷ Low.

Specifications: Brown paper sheets: 30 or 36 x 45 in (750 or 900 x 1,150 mm); rolls: 24, 30, 36, 40 and 48 in (600, 750, 900, 1,000 and 1,200 mm) wide; waxed in rolls 36 in (900 mm) wide.

WOOD • RUBBER, PLASTIC, RESIN & LINOLEUM • METAL • GLASS • FABRIC • **PAPER** • LEATHER • PAINT, VARNISH & LACQUER • STONE, CERAMICS & TILES • CONCRETE & CEMENT • PLASTER

CARD

INTERIOR MATERIALS & SURFACES: THE COMPLETE GUIDE

CARD

Plain, stiff card is an ideal material for making patterns, templates and shapes for tracing around when stenciling on walls or decorating window blinds. More decorative cards are used like veneers, to clad objects or fixtures, and are available in several thicknesses, with matte or gloss finishes, and in a wide range of pastel, bright or metallic colors.

Properties: Card stock is made by compressing paper fibers into a thick, stiff material to create a dense core. A thin sheet is then usually fused to either side, for protection, finish or decoration. This thin tissue paper surface is easily water damaged. Plastic-coated card is also available. As with art paper, finishes and textures can be smooth, finely ridged or styled like tweed, linen or silk. Glue card with water- or solvent-based glues; surfaces may darken in areas touched by wet glue.

Use and Maintenance: Card is widely used in picture framing, as mat board around the picture. A mat board's mitered trim exposes the card's core, so core color should be considered when choosing a mat board. It should also be acid-free. Linen card stock, although not very stiff usually 80lbs (170 or 180 grams per square meter), can provide an effective linen texture if attached to painted panels and screens, where paint would run or be absorbed by actual linen. Thick card is ideal for storage and filing boxes, using either colored card or plain card wrapped in decorative paper, and is often used for making innovatively shaped gift boxes. Card has a great many uses for stationery, crafts and bookmaking. It should be stored flat, out of direct sunlight, in a dry, temperate environment.

Safety and Environment: All card (except any with plasticized surfaces) will biodegrade easily with the combination of water and sunlight.

Availability: Small sheets are available from stationery stores. A wide range of full-size sheets can be sourced through specialized paper suppliers, artists' suppliers or graphic suppliers.

Cost: ❹ High.

Specifications: Large or small sheets for crafts. Card comes in weights from 90–140 lbs (200 gsm to 300 gsm) and up to mat board 110 lbs (600 gsm). Metallic card stock is about 107 lbs (290 gsm).

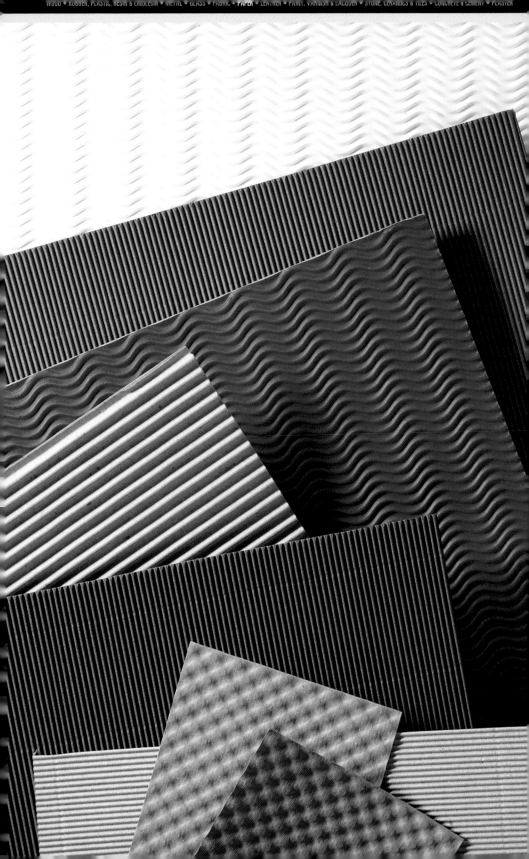

CORRUGATED PAPER

This utilitarian paper product has potential for a number of uses beyond cardboard boxes and packaging. Corrugated paper is much stronger than its flexible paper components and, for a paper product, it has great rigidity for its weight. This has led innovative designers to utilize it in the manufacture of furniture, and corrugated cardboard even plays a role in creating "living" outdoor furniture.

Properties: Corrugated paper or cardboard is usually constructed from mid-brown craft paper. The outer, facing sheets are of similar grade to the fluted interior, but are sometimes white. It is stiff, lightweight and rigid across its length. If faced on one side only, it can twist in parallel with the fluting to form folded or tubular shapes. Corrugated paper products are not moisture-resistant: any stretching or wrinkling caused by absorption is irreversible. A wax finish can improve water resistance, but once the end of the fibers or any inner surfaces are wet, the material disintegrates and loses structural ability.

Use and Maintenance: Corrugated paper's main use is in storage and filing boxes, and for packaging — moving companies use it for temporary containers for transporting hanging clothes. Corrugated paper is easily trimmed and folded or curved into shape, but is not suitable for paint finishes as the moisture weakens the fibers. Once

many layers have been laminated together, it can be cut using a hand- or power saw, and in this multilayered form it has been used as a structural element in architect-designed indoor furniture. The material's biodegradability has even been used for outdoor furniture; paper forms filled with soil and covered with turf can be used to make landform furniture. Eventually, the cardboard disappears, but the grassy furniture remains.

Safety and Environment: Corrugated cardboard is not meant to have a long life and will begin to biodegrade quickly when wet. It is easily recycled.

Availability: Small sheets of corrugated paper are available from stationery stores or artists' suppliers. Rolls of paper and larger sheets can be ordered from packaging manufacturers.

Cost: ❷ Low.

Specifications: Available in sheets (which can be waxed) or in rolls: 24, 30, 36, 40 or 48 in (600, 750, 900, 1,000 or 1,200 mm) wide. Waxed rolls are 36 in (900 mm) wide.

HANDMADE EXOTIC PAPER

The art of making handmade papers can be extended to produce truly exotic papers, decorated or worked using a variety of techniques, including embossing and layering, into exquisite designs. New technologies, such as mechanical embroidery, have added to the possibilities, creating a range of highly sophisticated papers. They are prized by craftspeople and can make eye-catching features in the home.

Properties: Decoration can take the form of embroidery, embossing (by hand or machine), crumpling and rolling for a random 3D effect, added ingredients such as petals or feathers, printed designs in colored inks or metallic paints, or distressing with water drops. Sheets of different colors fused together provide vibrant or subtle contrasting effects when folded or pleated to show both sides. The texture and strength of exotic papers depends on their plant components (see Traditional Handmade Papers, page 135), but they usually have the same features of durability, natural absorbency and resistance to insect attack. They are generally bleach-free, making them unaffected by sunlight. Papers can be acid-free unless toxic dyes or glues have been used in the decoration. Some papers are fabricated to be soft and floppy like cloth, although they cannot survive detergents or machine washing.

Use and Maintenance: Papers can be used unadorned or as a ground for further decoration.

Many papers are translucent, creating ideal screens and window coverings. Others make wonderful wallpaper, although matching pattern and grain will not be easy over a large area; the deckled edges can be overlapped or exposed as a feature. Stronger and heavier grades are perfect for making small storage units and decorative boxes.

Safety and Environment: These papers are either made from recycled materials or cultivated bushes and reeds that regenerate without difficulty. Raw materials are gathered and processed ecologically and products have a long life. Production processes often support local employment and help sustain ancient traditions.

Availability: Specialized paper importers and suppliers have a wide range; artists' suppliers stock smaller selections.

Cost: ❹ High.

Specifications: Sheets are usually 18 x 18 in (450 x 450 mm) and 20 x 30 in (500 x 750 mm). Some papers may be limited editions or unique items, so check availability when selecting.

WALLPAPER

Paper initially replaced fabric as a cheaper, easier-to-maintain wallcovering, and popular 18th-century papers mimicked expensive materials such as marble and velvet. Later patterns came to define an era, such as William Morris's Arts and Crafts designs. Although it fell out of fashion with the rise of minimalism at the end of the 20th century, wallpaper is enjoying a comeback in a newly romantic age.

Properties: Sophisticated processes ensure today's wallpapers have fade-resistant colors and patterns. Many are washable and, if laminated with a plastic coating, scrubbable. Use a paste recommended for the type and weight of paper being used; some papers are prepasted. Flocked paper, devised as a means of bringing a velvet texture to walls, is created by applying fine fabric fiber dust (cotton, silk, rayon or nylon) to a preglued pattern. Embossed, or anaglypta, wallpaper has a raised, textured effect and was originally made to emulate ceiling paneling or patterning.

Use and Maintenance: As well as an almost limitless range of printed patterns and subtle color washes, there are overall "picture panels" that can give the effect of a mural, and paper-backed seagrass and similar fibers are also available as wallpapers. Use plain lining paper to provide a smooth base on indoor walls for paintwork or papering (hang it at right angles, which usually means horizontally, as a base for a decorative top paper). Embossed papers can provide a pattern for embellishing with paintwork or disguise poor-quality wall surfaces. Matching borders can augment or replace the effect of crown molding, or make a transition at chair rail level between different patterns or finishes. Pattern-matching of large designs may involve much wastage, so allow for this when ordering.

Safety and Environment: Although wallpapers contain a high level of pigment, varnish and glue, they will biodegrade.

Availability: From decorating suppliers, home-improvement retailers or interior-design stores. Wallpaper is produced in batches (or dyed lots), so it is important to purchase your entire requirement in one order (and check batch numbers) to ensure the best match between rolls.

Cost: ❸–❹ Medium to high.

Specifications: Standard rolls 20½ in (520 mm) wide; some special papers up to 36 in (900 mm) wide, in lengths 12–20 ft (3.6–6 m).

CUSTOMIZED HANDMADE PAPER

Customized handmade papers are made by craftspeople using the historical techniques of papermaking developed in the Far East, but incorporating materials related to their local geography and landscape, such as twigs, dried leaves, flowers, herbs, indigenous fabrics or yarns and even gold, silver or copper leaf. This product is made to order and can be tailored to your requirements.

Properties: These papers are made by soaking gathered materials until soft (or "cooking" in an alkaline solution), beating the fibers together and pressing out the water before air drying. They often combine recycled materials, including paper, cotton and wool, with added color and textural elements. Custom-made papers intentionally highlight the diverse materials they are made of, so often have a varied texture, which can be coarse and rough. They are usually made with long fibers, which are not easily broken or damaged by water (although some pigments darken). Glues will soak into the open texture, forming a dark or shiny spot.

Use and Maintenance: As with other handmade papers, customized paper can be used unadorned or as a base for further decoration. They make effective screens, blinds or lampshades (intact or with perforated patterning). They can be used for wallpaper, but long rolls are not produced, so care is required to match grain and pattern over large areas. They are very strong; heavier grades are stiff and can be used to fabricate storage units or boxes. Finer grades are ideal for covering plain base materials. Wider applications include picture framing, stationery, arts and crafts and bookmaking.

Safety and Environment: Customized paper production often supports local employment in areas of little economic activity and helps sustain ancient traditions. It also makes use of waste products and employs natural materials, which will biodegrade.

Availability: Directly from artists or craftspeople. Some stationery suppliers may be in contact with papermakers.

Cost: ❸–❹ Medium to high.

Specifications: Sized to order, but sheets are handworked so cannot exceed an arm's length (22 x 30 in/ 550 x 750 mm). Order the correct amount — it will be impossible to rematch the design exactly.

LEATHER

The process of tanning leather for domestic use is one of the oldest industrial activities, and a Roman tannery has been unearthed in Pompeii. Early hunter-gatherers utilized the pelts of the animals they hunted to cover themselves for protection and modesty, as well as to provide a modicum of warmth and comfort as rudimentary furnishings and shelters. Raw animal hides, however, become stiff at low temperatures and rot in the heat, so, by trial and error, the tanning process gradually emerged as basic ways were found of softening, strengthening and preserving animal skins. The first simple tanning technique was to rub animal fat into the leather, and evidence of this is recorded in Homer's *Iliad*. Other preservation methods included drying in the sun, dehydrating with the use of salt, formaldehyde tanning with smoke from green leaves and twigs, and alum tanning using a mineral commonly found in volcanic areas.

Many cultures throughout the world developed the use of leather. Evidence has been found of clothing, including gloves and footwear, in ancient Egypt and Rome, and indigenous cultures across the globe. In addition to clothing, leather was used to make permanent and temporary shelters, furniture, vessels to carry water or belongings, waterproof coverings for boats and early inflatable flotation devices. The Phoenicians even used it for water pipes. Leather thongs were used as bindings to tie tools and structures

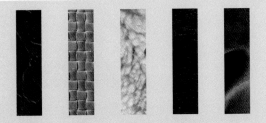

together and as harnessing for beasts of burden. Gradually, developments in tanning saw refinements in finishing processes to improve leather's appearance, malleability and strength. Nowadays, although modern chemicals and techniques mean leather can be processed in a matter of weeks rather than months, its appearance and uses have changed little.

Leather has always been used for a combination of utilitarian and decorative objects and often with highly decorative finishing. Many of the leather products we use today, from luggage, purses and shoes to upholstery, fastenings and trim, have been produced throughout the ages and it may be this connection with the past as well as the natural, tactile character of leather that makes it such a desirable material.

Leather has great potential as a floorcovering, with specialized manufacturers now producing very thick, regular tiles, or for lining walls or facing doors or cabinets. Hides and fleeces are perennially popular as throws and rugs. Fine finishing and tooling have allowed everyday items to be elevated with craftsmanship to art objects, and for a basic leather such as cowhide to be transmogrified into exotica such as alligator and lizard. There are alternative materials available to replace most traditional uses for leather, but as the raw material is a byproduct of the meat industry, there is always an opportunity to develop new products.

HIDE TILES

Leather has an association with luxury, and the individuality of a hide's particular nap and markings gives it a natural beauty that cannot be replicated with a synthetic substitute. Cutting hide into regular tile shapes enables this deluxe material to be laid on floors and walls, where it can be made to look traditional or highly contemporary and with time will acquire a deep patina.

Properties: Leather tiles are made from the hides of beef cattle. Each skin is individual, with particular grains, blemishes and brands, so the delivered product is unlikely to match a small sample exactly. Tiles are strong and long-lasting, and although the surface will scratch and scuff, it will eventually wear into a rich patina. Hide tiles are warm, smooth, soft to the touch, naturally antistatic and acoustic, readily absorbing airborne and vibrating sound. They deteriorate when exposed to moisture and will fade or discolor in direct sunlight.

Use and Maintenance: Leather tiles can be used on floors or walls for a soft, expensive effect, but are less suitable for rooms where they would encounter moisture or grease (although there are now leather tiles available that are water-resistant). Tiles are processed in batches; order a batch lot with a slight overrun to ensure a good match. Edges are smooth and should butt closely together. Before fitting, arrange in the area to be covered so that natural variation can be considered, and acclimatize for five or six days to avoid shrinkage or expansion after fitting. Any initial protective coating will wear off in time; reseal intermittently with beeswax. Vacuum often, wiping as necessary (especially spills) with a damp cloth. Never use solvent cleaners such as benzine or acetone, and, before cleaning, test any treatment first on an inconspicuous area.

Safety and Environment: Leather tiles are a byproduct of the food industry (from animals raised for meat or milk), so are an environmentally economic product as they make use of what would otherwise be a waste product.

Availability: Through specialized interior-design stores and flooring outlets. Suppliers offer standard colors and, usually, custom coloring to order.

Cost: ❺ Very high.

Specifications: Tile size generally 4 x 8 in (100 x 200 mm) or 12 x 12 in (300 x 300 mm), in thicknesses of ⅛ or ¹⁄₁₆ in (3.5 or 4.5 mm).

STAMPED AND EMBOSSED LEATHER

Leather can be embossed with a raised design that may be decorative, such as a geometric or paisley pattern, or imitate the characteristics of an exotic or fragile skin, such as alligator. Stamped and embossed leather was historically used in bookbinding, luggage, wallets and cowboy riding saddles, and embossing and stamping with gold edging is a traditional finish for desktops.

Properties: The fine, beautifully grained leathers originally used by the Moors for embossing were from goatskin (and came to be known as morocco, sought after for bookbinding), but the most commonly used leather for stamping and embossing is cowhide. It is prepared, stretched, moistened and then compressed between a patterned die and a layer of hard rubber. Areas can then be painted, prior to dyeing. Leather does not fray, but edges require skiving (finishing): either folding and beating with a mallet to compress the extra thickness, or polishing with glass or stone to close the pores and harden the surface.

Use and Maintenance: Thicker leathers can be stamped and used for decorative bowls, magazine racks and storage boxes, while thinner leathers are more appropriate for covering furniture or decorative objects. Leather can also be used to upholster walls or partitions, either directly onto the surface or stretched over foam for a padded effect. Leather is not suitable for areas of high moisture as exposure to dampness will gradually open the pores and damage it. Embossing leaves a smooth, shiny surface that can be wiped clean, and spills will not cause damage if wiped up promptly (those that sit will stain). Do not use solvent cleaners, and test cleaning treatments on an inconspicuous area. Do not store leather articles in airtight plastic.

Safety and Environment: Leather is a byproduct of the food industry, so it makes use of what would otherwise be a waste product.

Availability: Through specialized leather suppliers. A number of textures and colors are available.

Cost: ❹ High, usually varying with public demand for meat.

Specifications: Sizes available dependent on the animal from which the leather is derived. A cow's hide usually provides 48–60 sq ft (4.5–5.5 m²) of leather.

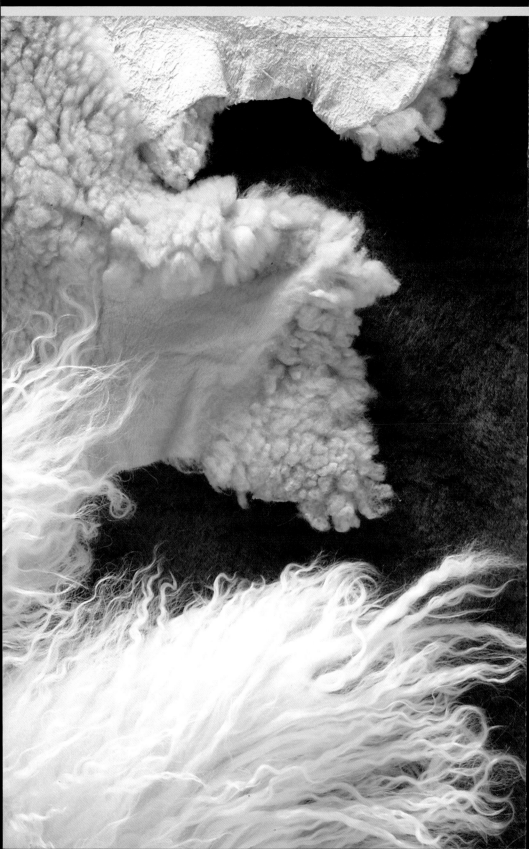

SHEEPSKIN

 Sheepskins are removed intact from sheep that are processed for food, so the fleece retains its natural leather backing. Once cleaned and combed, the fleeces can be dyed either a naturalistic color, such as champagne or brown-black, or fun shades from bright blue to pink or red. A sheepskin fleece is a cozy, insulating material, used for baby blankets and clothing as well as cushions and rugs.

Properties: Fleece is a natural insulator; warm in winter, cool in summer. Maintaining its original skin makes a fleece longer-lasting than one with a separate backing (see page 121), and improves its insulation qualities. Fleeces that are not dyed are usually bleached to give a more uniform appearance and the familiar ivory color. Wool is hypoallergenic. Like other natural fibers, it readily holds dyes and absorbs/desorbs water. When wet it has a detectable aroma and mildews if left damp. It absorbs airborne sound for a muffling effect and is naturally flame-retardant due to its high moisture and nitrogen content.

Use and Maintenance: Fleece on natural sheepskin backing is used for cushion covers and occasional rugs (often for fireplaces). Rugs can be original brushed wool in the shape of a hide, several hides sewn together to increase size or cut into rectangles, trimmed and dyed as "designer sheepskin." Other uses include throws, bedspreads, automobile seat covers and pet beds. Fleece wall hangings and throws generate a cozy atmosphere. Special fleece rugs with extra antibacterial treatment are produced for use as safe, comforting liners for baby cribs, strollers or as a mattress liner to alleviate bedrest problems. Hand-wash natural fleece products in warm, soapy water and air-dry. Protect exposed fibers from dust and vacuum regularly.

Safety and Environment: Sheepskins are a byproduct of the food industry and are a natural, biodegradable material. They can reduce levels of contaminants released in the home.

Availability: Natural fleeces are available from leather suppliers and some fabric stores. Rugs can be bought from carpet stores, specialized dealers and department stores. Sheepskin products are available from specialists or department stores.

Cost: ❹ High.

Specifications: Single sheepskins are about 3 x 3½ ft (925 x 1,050 mm) and 2½ in (65 mm) thick. Rugs and throws can be single or multiple hides.

WOOD • RUBBER, PLASTIC, RESIN & LINOLEUM • METAL • GLASS • FABRIC • PAPER • **LEATHER** • PAINT, VARNISH & LACQUER • STONE, CERAMICS & TILES • CONCRETE & CEMENT • PLASTER

PRINTED SKIN

INTERIOR MATERIALS & SURFACES: THE COMPLETE GUIDE

PRINTED SKIN

Printed skins are leathers that have been treated — bleached, trimmed and dyed — to give the appearance of a different animal or for an exotic effect. They can combine the natural beauty and qualities of leather with striking or outrageous features that are more instantly associated with synthetic products. Printed skins may be hairy or hairless and are treated to create alternative textures as well as colors.

Properties: Cowhides are often used to produce printed skins as they are durable and tear-resistant. Both textured and hairy hides are printed, either with natural dyes or intense, graduated or metallic colors. Cowhides lose their natural texture when dyed, so must be embossed (see page 155). Skins are finished with pigments and textures both to disguise imperfections and to ensure the surface is easily cleaned; it can be buffed to a shiny glaze or be matte or waxy. Leather's natural porosity means it absorbs moisture and traps pockets of air, helping to insulate against cold. Leather may dry or crack if kept too near high heat. It is naturally moldable and will hold a shape. Dyes and colors may fade in bright sunlight.

Use and Maintenance: Animal hides with hair can be colored with random patterns or made to resemble other animal hides, from zebra and giraffe to predators such as cheetah or snow leopard. Shorn hides can be textured to look like fish, ostrich skin, snake, lizard or crocodile. Printed skins are used for fitted upholstery, cushions, throws, hangings and, if reinforced, for bowls, storage boxes and similar household items. Protect them from water, which can alter the pigment and texture if allowed to soak in. Test any cleaning treatments on an inconspicuous area before use, and never use solvent cleaners such as benzine or acetone.

Safety and Environment: Cowhide is a byproduct of the food industry, so printed hides make use of what would otherwise be a waste product.

Availability: Through specialized leather suppliers, as upholstery through interior designers or furniture outlets and as accessories from gift and department stores.

Cost: ❹ High, usually varying with public demand for meat.

Specifications: Size is limited by the dimensions of the skin: a cow's hide usually provides 48–60 sq ft (4.5–5.5 m^2) of leather.

SUEDE

Suede is leather that has been treated with an abrasive action in order to break up the surface, thus creating a velvety texture. Like velvet, it will show slight color variations when the nap is brushed in different directions. Suede leather is a soft and luxurious material for upholstery, accessories and clothing, appreciated for its tactile qualities.

Properties: Suede leathers are usually cowhides, which are durable and tear-resistant. Suede is produced from the under layer of the hide (where skin contacts fleshy tissue), which is split from the upper, outer layer, then aniline dyed and buffed. Even apparently natural colors will have been dyed to disguise the variable pigmentation of the original skin. Suede retains leather's porous and moisture-absorbent nature, making it a good insulator. Like other leathers, it is moldable and will hold a shape. Dyes may fade if exposed to bright sunlight.

Use and Maintenance: Suede is available in many natural, pale and bright colors. Its main use in the home is as upholstery and accessories such as cushions, throws and patchworked rugs, but it can also be used as wall paneling (stretched over board, foam or drapes) or for covering picture frames and storage boxes. The surface should be protected from stains and spills as much as possible; it can be treated with a proprietary water and stain repellant. Always test cleaning treatments on an inconspicuous area first and never use solvent or spot cleaners (such as benzine or acetone). Do not store suede articles in airtight plastic. Although moisture should not be allowed to penetrate leathers, suede can be rehabilitated by steaming and brushing up the nap with a soft, bristled brush while damp.

Safety and Environment: Suede is a byproduct of the food industry, so it makes use of a product that would otherwise go to waste.

Availability: Suedes can be sourced through leather suppliers and some fabric stores, as upholstery from interior designers or furniture outlets, and accessories from a variety of gift and department stores.

Cost: ❹ High, usually varying with public demand for meat.

Specifications: Dimensions are dependent on the size of the particular animal used.

PAINT, VARNISH & LACQUER

Paint has been used as a decorative element since the Stone Age, when a mixture of animal fat and plant dyes was used to depict scenes of successful hunts or dreams of the afterlife on the walls of cave dwellings. The ancient Greeks and Romans painted frescoes on the walls of palaces and houses. In the Middle Ages churches were adorned with paintings and frescoes, and paint emerged as a decorative material on interior and exterior walls of ordinary domestic dwellings.

To begin with, paintwork in houses was limited to the application of a fresh, clean surface coat such as whitewash, which could be applied to crude plaster or stone walls. This had to be renewed regularly and was regarded as a practical housekeeping chore rather than a form of embellishment. Later, dyes and pigments were added, along with increasingly sophisticated binding agents, to allow a greater range of textures and colors and a longer-lasting finish.

From about 1700 onward, paint was produced for the domestic market in Europe and North America, and paint effects were often used to mimic other materials. Paint enabled plaster walls or wood moldings to be finished to appear like sculpted marble or stone. Decorative painting techniques such as rag rolling, sponging, marbling, stenciling, glazing and crackling were developed, making use of combinations of paints, glazes and varnishes

to produce a range of decorative effects. Nowadays modern paints are available in literally every color under the sun, and computer analysis to match exact shades of, say, fabrics or old paint finishes, is widely available.

In its early form, varnish was a utilitarian preservative and protective coating for wood, mostly for ships, where there is evidence that it has been in use since the ninth century. Early varnishes were made of natural oils to penetrate the wood and resins to seal it, and although modern varnishes often contain synthetic components and additives to increase performance, they work on very similar principles. Varnish- and oil-based preservatives are now often selected in preference to opaque paint finishes on wood, to reveal the underlying wood, which has become increasingly valued for its natural warmth, grain and texture.

New sealants are continually being developed to offer combinations of natural and synthetic components to enhance the appearance of base materials, to provide high-quality coatings that entirely mask a base material or to give superior wear for durable, long-lasting weatherproofing. As well as paints for wood and plaster, there are paints specifically formulated for metals, glass and ceramic, rough concrete, fabrics and even to give new life to plastics.

APPLIANCE PAINT

When kitchen appliances are scuffed beyond the point of wiping clean but are not yet in need of replacing, they can be freshened up with a coat of specially formulated paint, which gives a very smooth finish and durable new surface. Appliance paint is suitable for all kitchen appliances, with the exception of stove tops, ovens and the interiors of microwave ovens.

Properties: This paint provides either a metallic luster or white, brushed-on finish. It is almost as tough and hard wearing as factory-finished stove enamel. The quality of the finish depends on the appliance's surface condition. Final texture can be made to match a factory finish by applying with a natural bristle roller. The paint is not rustproof, so should not be applied directly to exposed metal. It dries to the touch in two hours, can be overcoated in six hours and is completely dry in 12 hours. It will only adhere to scrupulously clean surfaces. Being solvent-based, it is flammable (as are any paint-soaked cloths). Use only in well-ventilated areas.

Use and Maintenance: This paint is intended as a finish to refresh tired-looking surfaces or to coordinate appliances of several different finishes. It is suitable for indoor use on enameled kitchen appliances, including refrigerators, freezers, washing machines, dishwashers and microwaves. It is not suitable for gas or convection ovens, stove tops or the insides of microwave ovens. Before painting, ensure appliances are cool and clean. Wipe surfaces with denatured alcohol, then with a wipe-on, multisurface primer to ensure the paint adheres properly. Cover any exposed metal, plastic trim or handles with painter's tape. Apply two coats, allowing appropriate drying time in line with instructions, and sanding lightly between each coat.

Safety and Environment: Do not dispose of paint into drains or soil. Local waste collectors may take away large quantities of leftover paint by special arrangement. Leave cans open until the paint dries; the paint can then be scraped out and the cans recycled. Partially empty aerosol containers must be disposed of as hazardous waste.

Availability: From home-improvement retailers, paint and wallpaper stores and building suppliers.

Cost: ❸ Medium.

Specifications: Available in spray form in 12 oz (354 ml) aerosol cans. Use in conjunction with wipe-on multisurface primer, available from the same suppliers.

MELAMINE PAINT

Painting existing kitchen units, cupboard doors, kitchen tables and chairs is a cost-effective way of giving your kitchen a face-lift without the expense of replacing anything except a few handles. This satin-finish paint was specifically developed for smooth, nonporous surfaces such as melamine, which are traditionally difficult to cover with paints formulated for wood or metal and cannot be prepared by sanding.

Properties: Melamine paint is tough and durable, with reasonable resistance to knocks and abrasion. It is intended for melamine or similar plastic-covered kitchen units, cupboards and furniture. It may also be suitable for other plastic surfaces; test prior to application. Do not use on countertops or on laminated or woodstrip floors. It is not suitable for use outdoors. This paint is flammable (as are paint-soaked cloths or rags). Use only in well-ventilated areas.

Use and Maintenance: A tired-looking kitchen that has structurally sound units and a good layout but is superficially shabby can be revitalized with a few coats of melamine paint. Use it on any smooth, melamine-coated surface — furniture and bookshelves as well as cupboard doors and frames. Most melamine paints require a priming coat and one or two topcoats. Some have a self-priming component, but even these perform better over a primer; choose a wipe-on, multisurface or melamine primer. For a wider color selection, other solvent-based topcoats may be used over a melamine primer, but test for compatibility first. To prepare, remove all ironwork (filling holes if new handles are of a different size), clean with a cream cleanser, then wipe with denatured alcohol. Allow coats to dry at least as long as specified on the can. Lightly sand and wipe clean before applying topcoats.

Safety and Environment: Do not dispose of paint into drains or soil. Local waste collectors may take away large quantities of leftover paint by special arrangement. Leave cans open until paint dries; paint can then be scraped out and the cans recycled.

Availability: From industrial paint suppliers, building centers and home-improvement retailers.

Cost: ❸ Medium.

Specifications: In 1 qt (750 ml or 1 l) cans, also available in gallon cans. Limited color range (about 8 pastel colors).

CERAMIC TILE PAINT

Ceramic wall tiles in kitchens and bathrooms are long-lasting, but colors and patterns go in and out of style, so tile paint can be an effective way of updating tiling without the upheaval and expense of replacing it. Ceramic tile paints are easy to apply on interior tiles with a high-gloss and satin finish, quickly providing a fresh look or a change of color.

Properties: Tile paint primer is a low-odor, water-based paint that acts as an adhesive undercoat for tile paints or other high-performance, solvent-based gloss or satin paints. Ceramic tile paints are easy to apply, quick-drying, tough, hard-wearing and abrasion-resistant. They are not suitable for use on tiled floors, countertops or outdoor areas, and should not be used in conjunction with water-based or emulsion paints (the water-based tile primer is an exception). Tile paints are flammable, as are any paint-soaked cloths or rags. Use all paints in a well-ventilated area.

Use and Maintenance: Tile paint can be used on glass as well as ceramic wall tiles, and is suitable for areas that get wet, such as shower enclosures, although the paint must not be applied in damp or cold conditions. Clean off grime, mineral deposits, grease and other contaminants, and wash tiles with a cream cleanser, then wipe with denatured alcohol before painting. Primer provides an adhesive surface to aid the application of topcoats; even single-coat paints perform better with a primer. If applying more than one coat of paint, sand the surface between applications. Paints are often supplied with a grout-cleaning or -painting product, but scraping out and reapplying grout is advisable. Various pigments for coloring grout to coordinate with tiles are available.

Safety and Environment: Do not dispose of paint into drains or soil. Local waste collectors may take away large quantities of leftover paint by special arrangement. Leave cans open until the paint dries; paint can then be scraped out and the cans recycled.

Availability: From home-improvement retailers and building suppliers. Grout, grout paint and grout pigments are stocked by tile and home-improvement retailers.

Cost: ❸ Medium.

Specifications: Tile primer and paint: 1 qt (750 ml and 1 or 2 l) cans. About 10 colors of one-coat paint, 15 topcoat colors.

WOOD • RUBBER, PLASTIC, RESIN & LINOLEUM • METAL • GLASS • FABRIC • PAPER • LEATHER • PAINT, VARNISH & LACQUER • STONE, CERAMICS & TILES • CONCRETE & CEMENT • PLASTER

HIGH-PERFORMANCE EXTERIOR GLOSS

INTERIOR MATERIALS & SURFACES: THE COMPLETE GUIDE

HIGH-PERFORMANCE EXTERIOR GLOSS

Various high-performance coatings have been specially developed to create highly durable, hard-wearing, all-weather surface finishes. In many of these finishes, the use of epoxy resins in their makeup allows them to be applied directly in all but the most extreme weather conditions. These paints are most commonly used to extend the performance of exterior gloss paints from two years up to seven years.

Properties: Performance of these paints depends on the use of epoxy resin. They have various viscosities, from thick to water-thin. They are corrosion-resistant, chemical- and mildew-resistant, tolerant of high temperatures, hard, tough and abrasion- and stain-resistant. Some are impact-resistant. Some can be used to coat steel immersed in water. Coatings are low maintenance and easy to reapply. Their integral flexibility allows for expansion and contraction of the surface beneath without causing cracking or flaking. Eggshell- and satin-finished products are available in a low-maintenance category known as HIPAC (high-performance architectural coating), for use in zones prone to severe weather.

Use and Maintenance: A variety of products with specific applications exists. Uses include areas of high traffic or extreme moisture (such as three- or four-piece bathrooms) and rustproofing for metal (including below water). They will give a smooth finish to concrete walls or floors, filling the open texture and surface faults. They will provide protection for structural steel, piping and equipment, and are suitable for recoating and protecting pitted steel surfaces. They can also be applied to glazed bricks and exterior-grade ceramic tiles. Some products are designed for one-coat application; others require a primer and two coats with sanding in between. For lumber, use products that are moisture-vapor permeable or microporous so that moisture does not build up within the lumber and cause rot.

Safety and Environment: Do not dispose of paint into drains or soil. Local waste collectors may take away large quantities of leftover paint by special arrangement. Leave cans open until the paint dries; paint can then be scraped out and the cans recycled.

Availability: Through home-improvement retailers, paint and wallpaper stores and building suppliers.

Cost: ❹ High.

Specifications: In quart or gallon (1, 2 or 2.5 l) cans.

HIGH-GLOSS ENAMEL

These traditional solvent-based paints give a rich, glossy look and opaque, hard-wearing finish to wooden doors and trim, metal, concrete and masonry. Their density of color and their excellent color retention make them ideal for exposed, sunlit positions where color fade would be a problem. The best finish is achieved by applying several thin coats, sanding between each coat.

Properties: Although enamels generally have excellent color retention, some white and lighter colors yellow over time (others contain an additive that prevents this). Enamels should be used with an enamel primer. They are tough, long-wearing and abrasion- and weather-resistant. They also resist detergents. Do not apply in damp conditions or at temperatures below 50°F (10°C). Solvents have toxic vapors, so should be applied in well-ventilated areas. Paints (and paint-soaked cloths) are highly flammable. Enamels irritate skin and eyes and are harmful or fatal if swallowed.

Use and Maintenance: Enamels are versatile; use on wooden doors, window frames, trim, exterior wooden siding, furniture, machinery, iron, steel, aluminum, masonry, brickwork and concrete walls. Ferrous metals should be treated with rust inhibitor before priming. Ensure new concrete is fully cured before painting. These paints can either be applied to previously painted or to properly primed surfaces.

Before priming, ensure surfaces are free of flaking paint and dust. Sand wood thoroughly before painting, and between each coat, wiping clean of dust. Allow priming coats to dry overnight before their first enamel coat. Some enamels are specially formulated for floors. Continue to stir paint during application as the pigment separates and sinks to the bottom. Enamels are tack-free in about four hours, but allow to dry overnight before recoating. Use mineral spirits to thin the paint.

Safety and Environment: Do not dispose of paint into drains or soil. Local waste collectors may take away large quantities of leftover paint by special arrangement. Leave cans open until the paint dries; paint can then be scraped out and the cans recycled.

Availability: From decorating and building suppliers and home-improvement retailers.

Cost: ❸ Medium.

Specifications: In quart or gallon (500 ml and 1, 2.5 or 5 l) cans. White, black and about 12 ready-mixed colors available.

MILK PAINT

Historically, milk paints were made from milk protein (calcium caseinate from skim milk or buttermilk), mixed with crushed limestone and various pigments, for painting wooden furniture and interior moldings in colonial North America. Today water-based paints produced to replicate an authentic milk-paint finish are particularly suited to re-creating, for example, a colonial or Shaker look.

Properties: These water-soluble paints are intended for use directly on wooden surfaces. Certain high-tech milk paints provide a high-quality satin sheen, replicating an old-fashioned finish. Original coloring came from a variety of sources, from earth pigments to chimney soot. Pigs' blood produced the deep, vibrant red associated with some communities. Milk paints have a slight odor when wet (this disappears when dry). They contain no lead, petroleum derivatives, chemical preservatives or fungicides. Although classed as nontoxic paints, some of the natural substances used for coloring (iron oxide and lampblack) are not desirable ingestants. Pigments are long-lasting, but fade in direct sunlight.

Use and Maintenance: Milk paints can be applied to raw wood, but a primer enhances performance. They are used for furniture, cabinets and some outdoor furniture. Wood should be sanded thoroughly before painting, and between each coat, and rubbed down to remove dust. Authentic milk paints will be made from natural products and available in powder form (to be mixed with water). Colors can be mixed to obtain different hues. Repeated coats build up into a deep, creamy color; diluted paint will give a distressed, stained look; dry paintwork can be rubbed down for a burnished, semigloss finish. A gelatin-based glaze can be applied for a crackled, antique appearance.

Safety and Environment: Modern water-based milk paints are safe and nontoxic, so can be used for children's toys and furniture or in homes where people may be allergic to chemical paints.

Availability: Through specialized paint suppliers and furniture makers.

Cost: ❸ Medium.

Specifications: In powdered form (to be mixed with water) in about 16 premixed colors, but these can be mixed with each other or with acrylic pigments.

FLOOR PAINT

Floor paints provide a tough, durable new surface to concrete, stone, brick or wood floors or other porous, hard-wearing surfaces. They are intended for use in areas where they will encounter scuffing, scraping and heavy wear, such as laundry rooms, sunrooms, basements and storerooms, but are an appropriate coating wherever a flat, cleanable surface is desired.

Properties: The quality of a painted floor depends on its substrate; ensure flooring is sound and in good condition. Paints are intended for bare or previously painted porous surfaces. Floor paints are solvent-based; use in well-ventilated areas. They do not reach true hardness for five or six days, so allow to cure for the full period. If used in damp or cold conditions, gloss formation may be affected and drying time lengthened. Floor paints are slippery when wet. Rising moisture can lift painted surfaces. Paints are flammable.

Use and Maintenance: Paint should be applied to clean, dry surfaces. New concrete should dry for at least one month before covering. New concrete develops a brittle top surface when drying; break this down with a wire brush, clean and apply sealant. Brick or stone should also be wire-brushed to remove loose material, then sealed. Bare or painted wood should be sanded and knot sealant applied. Some quick-drying floor paints can have two coats applied in a day, but it is important to follow the exact prescribed time intervals (always consult the manufacturer's instructions). Certain floor paints are formulated for use on vinyl floors, and specific products exist for garage floors, front steps and thresholds. Some can be used indoors and out. Floor paints are not suitable for ceramic, terra-cotta or quarry floor tiles, or asphalt.

Safety and Environment: Do not dispose of paint into drains or soil. Local waste collectors may take away large quantities of leftover paint by special arrangement. Leave cans open until the paint dries; the paint can then be scraped out and the cans recycled.

Availability: From home-improvement retailers, paint and wallpaper stores and building suppliers.

Cost: ❸ Medium.

Specifications: In quart or gallon (750 ml and 2.5 l) cans in about 12 colors; limited colors are also available in quart or gallon (250 ml or 5 l) cans.

YACHT ENAMEL

Yacht enamel is a high-performance polyurethane, used primarily as a rust-preventative, decorative finish on metals subject to wet but not submerged conditions. It dries to a rock-hard, nonporous finish that should not chip, crack or peel. It is useful for railings, lampposts, machinery and steel trim. It is also used for protecting metal fixtures on roofs and for repairing damage to boats and automobiles.

Properties: Properties vary with color: silver contains metal fillers and is suitable for heavily pitted areas; clear enamel gives the smoothest finish. Some are cured and strengthened by exposure to moisture and dry faster under extreme humidity. Others are sensitive to UV in sunlight. Cans should be stirred (not shaken) to mix settled pigment. Enamels will not burn the skin but will stain immediately and are toxic. They are impervious to fuels, battery acids and oils. They are solvent-based, so wear a mask and work in a well-ventilated area.

Use and Maintenance: Yacht enamels can be painted directly onto rusted or seasoned (i.e., not new) metal surfaces once they have been cleaned. Clean protective oil finishes from new metals before enameling. These enamels must be used with compatible preprimers, primers and topcoats. Use preprimers to remove loose rust and neutralize base metal. In addition to using as fillers for pitted or damaged metal, enamels can be used as concrete floor paint (once the concrete is properly cured), and on putty or fiberglass. Fiberglass cloth can be used to patch holes, for example in a boat or automobile body, before overpainting with enamel. Enamels must be applied to clean, dry surfaces in dry conditions, but cure best in a moist atmosphere. Topcoats should be fully cured prior to exposure to prolonged sunlight.

Safety and Environment: It is advisable to calculate how much is required so as not to overorder. Enamel should be dried in the open can before disposal.

Availability: From specialized paint suppliers, boat and automobile suppliers and building centers.

Cost: ❹ High.

Specifications: In quart or gallon (500 ml and 1, 2.5 or 5 l) cans in silver, gloss and semigloss black, gray and clear.

WOOD • RUBBER, PLASTIC, RESIN & LINOLEUM • METAL • GLASS • FABRIC • PAPER • LEATHER • **PAINT, VARNISH & LACQUER** • STONE, CERAMICS & TILES • CONCRETE & CEMENT • PLASTER

ORGANIC PAINT

INTERIOR MATERIALS & SURFACES: THE COMPLETE GUIDE

ORGANIC PAINT

Organic paints are made entirely from natural and organic materials in an effort to reduce the impact on the environment of synthetic products. They are chosen primarily for their ecological qualities, rather than cost, performance or color selection, and are more expensive to the consumer due to rigorous standards of organic procurement, lower market share and the direct costs of research and development.

Properties: Organic is not the same as nontoxic (many nontoxic paints are unecologically produced). Organic paints are ecologically acceptable and made without using petrochemicals. Modern organic paints strive to be nontoxic, but some produced by traditional methods contain toxic ingredients, such as lead. Nontoxic paints are labeled as such. Most organic paints are low-odor, but should be applied in ventilated areas. Many are water-based. Gloss paints are made with natural resin. Pigment in organic stains protects wood from UV rays; natural borax prevents fungus and insect damage. Many paints are microporous, allowing the material beneath to breathe. Some meet vegan standards.

Use and Maintenance: A full range of organic paint finishes are produced for interior and exterior use on various surfaces, as well as lacquers, waxes and oils. Organic products feel different from synthetics; if you have not used them before, do a test to experience their application and appearance prior to starting your project. Surfaces previously painted with other paints will have to be stripped or primed with appropriate products. Paint colors are mixed per batch and will not necessarily match exactly, so unless purchased directly from the manufacturer in a set batch, it is useful to mix paint from each can, so the end color is uniform. Nontoxic paints are suitable for children's toys and furniture.

Safety and Environment: Organic paints are made entirely from natural materials, and producers will be part of a certification program to ensure their products meet eco-friendly, organic criteria.

Availability: From ecological building suppliers or decorators, certain specialized paint suppliers and some organic food stores. Availability will increase as demand grows.

Cost: ❹ High.

Specifications: Primers, topcoats, lacquers, metal paints and all topcoat finishes (gloss, matte, eggshell, etc.) in sample pots in quart or gallon (750 ml and 2 or 5 l) cans; wood stains in about 20 colors.

WOOD • RUBBER, PLASTIC, RESIN & LINOLEUM • METAL • GLASS • FABRIC • PAPER • LEATHER • **PAINT, VARNISH & LACQUER** • STONE, CERAMICS & TILES • CONCRETE & CEMENT • PLASTER

VARNISH

INTERIOR MATERIALS & SURFACES: THE COMPLETE GUIDE

VARNISH

Varnishes are intended as a transparent sealant for lumber and wood products to protect against damage from moisture, staining, wear or weather while preserving the natural appearance of the wood. They have a gloss, satin or matte finish. Tinted varnishes can give a subtle or rich cast to the color of the wood beneath without obscuring the grain or other features.

Properties: Wood varnishes are made up of oil, solvents, thinners, resins, dryers, additives and UV inhibitors. Varnishes can be clear, tinted in natural colors or pigmented with dark or bright colors. Some contain flattening paste, to give a satin or matte finish; this clouds appearance and produces a slightly less durable finish. Most varnishes are solvent-based, highly flammable and should be used in a well-ventilated area. They have good resistance to abrasion, wear, solvents and water vapor. Varnishes warm or darken lumber when applied; many yellow further with age. Unless specifically formulated, they take considerable time to dry.

Use and Maintenance: Different varnishes give varying moisture-proofing, elasticity or UV protection. Yacht varnish, for instance, protects against sea- and fresh water and weather conditions, so makes an ideal hardy exterior varnish. The flattening agent in satin and matte varnishes also softens the finish, so if an extremely hard-wearing finish is required without a deep gloss, choose gloss varnish and rub down the last coat with steel wool, then buff to give a satin sheen. Satin or matte varnishes also have a cloudy effect after several coats, so to preserve the clarity of the wood, build up sealant in gloss coats, using matte or satin only for the final coats. Varnishes are usually applied by brush. Allow to dry thoroughly between coats in dust-free conditions.

Safety and Environment: Do not dispose of varnish into drains or soil. Local waste collectors may take away large quantities of leftover product by special arrangement. Leave cans open until the varnish dries; it can then be scraped out and the cans recycled.

Availability: From decorating and building suppliers and home-improvement retailers.

Cost: ❸ Medium.

Specifications: Selections of varnish, based on pigment color, drying time and surface finish, are available in pint, quart or gallon (500 ml and 1, 2.5 or 5 l) cans.

LINSEED OIL

Oil applied to a natural or stained wood surface soaks into the wood, eventually hardening when exposed to the air (nondrying oils, such as mineral oils, should not be used as wood sealants). Oil preserves the original texture of the wood and helps to seal it from moisture, while providing a fine, natural finish. It gives a very pleasant look to wood floors, countertops and furniture.

Properties: Although sold as French, Danish and Dutch brands, oils for wood are usually a mixture of boiled linseed oil, turpentine and distilled white vinegar. Boiling the linseed accelerates drying time, as do additives, but oils are slow-drying. They are only water-resistant in low-moisture areas and linseed oil can promote mildew growth if wood remains damp. Oils are not usually UV-resistant, so will not protect against sunlight (this degrades surface fibers, facilitating fungus and insect attack). Oils penetrate wood, so are difficult to remove and replace with another finish. They are highly flammable: oil-soaked rags can spontaneously combust, so store in water in a metal container. Oils are skin irritants. Use in a well-ventilated area.

Use and Maintenance: Oils are unsuitable for external decking as they are not abrasion-resistant and require waxing to seal fully, which would make them extremely slippery when wet. Do not pour oil directly onto wood so it pools, or it will gum and become tacky; apply in thin coats with a lint-free cloth, rubbing with the grain, and allow to dry naturally. Oil finishes are easily retouched and need reapplying yearly. When replacing windowpanes, add linseed oil to putty to improve malleability, and rub it into lumber mullions prior to glazing to prevent the wood absorbing the putty's oil and drying it too fast.

Safety and Environment: Although linseed oil is made from a natural product, it also contains a variety of additives. The highly flammable nature of oils must be noted and care taken in use and storage.

Availability: From building and decorating suppliers and home-improvement retailers.

Cost: ❷ Low.

Specifications: In pint, quart or gallon (250 or 500 ml and 1, 2 or 2.5 l) cans or bottles.

HANDMADE PAINT

Handmade paints in the form of pigments in an encaustic wax or oil base have traditionally been made by and for artists since ancient times. They contain natural pigments — iron oxides, zinc, cobalt, copper, titanium dioxide, cadmium sulfides — many used by the old masters. These colors have gained evocative historical names: Prussian and Cobalt Blue, Cadmium Red and Yellow, Van Dyke Brown, Burnt Sienna.

Properties: Beeswax, pigment and resin are used to make these vivid, nonfading and nondarkening paints. Certain paints contain fragile pigments such as carmine or lapis lazuli, which cannot be treated by industrial methods. Pigment sticks, which contain pure pigment plus wax, are intended for direct application. They have a lipstick consistency with the fluidity, subtlety and durability of traditional oil paints. They are creamy, nondrip and slow-drying. Wax-based paints become brittle when dry, so require an absorbent, rigid surface. Tube paints contain pigment and drying oils (linseed) but no wax, so the consistency is more liquid. Pigment powder can be fine to granular (for a reflective effect). Colors are rich and intense, usually giving good coverage and a matte, velvety appearance. They can be built up into durable textured surfaces. Some paints are highly toxic.

Use and Maintenance: Handmade paints are clear, pure pigments intended for fine art or conservation work. Encaustic paint is a hot wax medium. The paints are heated on a hot plate before being applied with a brush, palette knife or fingers. They dry quickly, but reapplied heat will resoften. Several paints, once applied to the surface to be decorated, can be reheated to melt together and unite the layers for a fused effect. Use handmade paints on decorative surfaces for intense color or thick texture. Do not use on exterior surfaces.

Safety and Environment: Although made from natural products, these paints can be toxic. Once dry they are safe to handle, so allow to dry before disposal. Oil content makes products a fire risk, so store in a secure container.

Availability: From specialized art material suppliers, who will also stock associated products such as lead primers and rabbit skin size.

Cost: ❺ Very high.

Specifications: Sticks: 6½ x 1½ in (165 x 37 mm) diameter and 5 x ¾ in (125 x 21 mm) diameter. Encaustic paints: 4 or 12 fl oz (104 or 333 ml) blocks.

PVA PAINT

PVA (polyvinyl acetate) is a common polymer that is used in many wood glues and gives a shiny coating to paper and textiles. PVA paints are quick-drying, water-based paints that are used as topcoats, or as sealants or primers on porous surfaces to provide a smooth, uniform underlay that is not brittle or prone to cracking (artists use diluted PVAs to provide a ground or primer for canvases).

Properties: PVA is added to pigment and water as a binder, forming vinyl acrylic or latex paint. It bonds well with pigment, ensuring long-lasting color and a durable low-gloss sheen. PVA paints are water-soluble, but waterproof after curing. They are quick-drying and have a shiny, wipeable surface. They remain soluble in ethanol and other alcohols, but resist acids, alkalis and UV rays. They have low toxicity and low odor, but should be used in a well-ventilated area. They may irritate skin, eyes and lungs (use a mask when spraying). Most require a temperature above 50°F (10°C) during application. Long-term performance depends on pigment quality and additives used. Paints are nonflammable.

Use and Maintenance: PVA paints are intended for use on walls, not furniture nor, generally, wood; some have been formulated for external use, or for wood, vinyl and aluminum. Use PVA paints on interior stone, brick or concrete surfaces (allow new concrete a month to cure fully), and as an undercoat on untreated plaster or drywall to aid coverage and adhesion of the topcoat. Colors can be mixed, but do not thin paints; apply in supplied consistency. PVA paints are not intended for concealing stains or previously painted surfaces. Art conservators use PVA paints for infilling pigments, as they can be wiped away with alcohol without damaging original underlayers.

Safety and Environment: As with all paints, PVAs should be allowed to dry in the can prior to disposal along with household waste. Large amounts should be disposed of through local waste collectors as toxic waste.

Availability: From paint and decorating suppliers, building suppliers, home-improvement retailers and art material suppliers.

Cost: ❷ Low.

Specifications: In pint, quart and gallon (500 ml and 1, 2 or 5 l) cans in standard colors. Some colors are available for tinting to order.

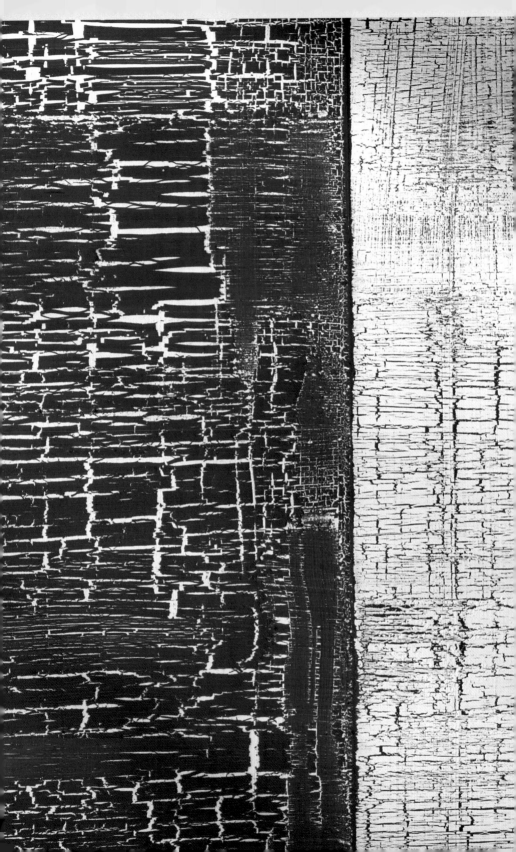

CRACKLE GLAZES

Crackle glazes — also known as crawl paints — are used to mimic the effects of climatic conditions or aging on old paints. This distinctive type of decorative finish is created by applying a sequence of specially formulated varnishes or paint products to produce a distressed, finely cracked, antique appearance. The effect is similar to craquelure, the pattern of hairline cracking found on old master paintings.

Properties: A crackled surface is achieved by two methods of applying layers of incompatible sealants. Crackle varnish lays a quick-drying, water-based varnish over a thin, slow-drying, oil-based glaze; as the lower layer dries and shrinks more slowly than the upper layer, cracks appear across the surface. Crackle medium uses an undercoat of hide glue followed (when dry) by a latex top layer. The cracked texture can be enhanced by the use of a hair dryer. Crackled surfaces have good resistance to abrasion, wear, solvents and water vapor. Varnishes warm or darken lumber slightly and many yellow further with age.

Use and Maintenance: Crackle glazes are intended for use on primed and painted wood surfaces. Pigments can be added to either the varnish layer or to the cracks that form after drying is complete (but prior to the finishing coat). When the crackle has cured, rub with a new layer of oil-based varnish to fill cracks and smooth the surface. Crackling is ideal for plain furniture or flat wall surfaces; on heavily ornate or deeply carved surfaces, the varnish will sit thickly in the recesses. It is very effective on painted wooden furniture, from tables and chairs to armoires, and on wooden picture and mirror frames. With the right primers, it can also be used on kitchen cabinets or ceramic tiles (see page 205).

Safety and Environment: Do not dispose of these products into drains or soil. Local waste collectors can take away large leftover quantities by special arrangement. Leave cans open until the product dries; it can then be scraped out and the cans recycled.

Availability: From art and craft suppliers, paint and decorating stores and home-improvement retailers.

Cost: ❸ Medium.

Specifications: Crackle varnish and crackle medium varnishes in kits with quart or gallon (300 ml and 1 or 4 l) cans.

STONE, CERAMICS & TILES

Blocks of stone, known as dimensional stone, have been quarried and used in construction since the pyramids were built in Egypt 4,500 years ago. Stone blocks are visible in the remains and ruins of the buildings of the ancient Greeks, and in Roman roads, which extended throughout the empire.

The properties of types of stone depend essentially on the way they have been formed. Igneous rocks, as the name implies, are forged in great heat, deep below the Earth's surface. The most common igneous rock used as a building material is granite. Sedimentary rocks, such as limestone, sandstone and travertine, are compressed sediments, laid down millennia ago by rivers and seas. These sometimes expose tiny fossils and shells. Metamorphic rocks, which include marble, quartzite and slate, vary in origin, but have all been transformed by additional pressures and stresses.

Marble and other sought-after stone has traditionally been expensive to quarry and transport. As new sources and new masonry techniques were developed and mechanized, however, and the skills necessary to work the stone spread beyond the boundaries of Italy where they originally developed, stone has emerged as an affordable material that can be used in many domestic applications where its beauty and durability are an asset. Even the use of marble for mosaics is enjoying a revival.

Like stone blocks, the use of ceramic tiles in buildings has historical roots. There is evidence of glazed ceramic tiles in ancient cultures from Babylon to Egypt. Tiles were used to create brilliant and lasting decoration, nowhere more creatively than in the Islamic culture in Persia where use and production methods were refined and perfected.

The use of brightly colored, embossed and geometric tiles spread to countries around the Mediterranean, but did not really extend into Europe until the 12th century. From then on styles proliferated: Italy produced richly colored and glazed maiolica tiles, craftsmen in Antwerp and Delft painted tiles in the same styles as their pottery tableware and iconographic tiles were typical in France, England and Germany. Spain, influenced by the Islamic tradition, had long been a major center for ceramic production and from the 16th century developed techniques that facilitated the first mass production of ceramic tiles. Spanish manufacturers still hold a pre-eminent position in tile production.

Ceramic and stone tiling can be used to create protective or decorative effects almost anywhere, from walls, floors and ceilings to fireplaces, murals and mosaics. Tiles are practical and attractive materials that can be used indoors and out, and in a range of styles, from sleek minimalist to multicolored Mediterranean and from luxurious and sophisticated to sturdily rustic.

WOOD • RUBBER, PLASTIC, RESIN & LINOLEUM • METAL • GLASS • FABRIC • PAPER • LEATHER • PAINT, VARNISH & LACQUER • STONE, CERAMICS & TILES • CONCRETE & CEMENT • PLASTER

LIMESTONE AND SANDSTONE

INTERIOR MATERIALS & SURFACES: THE COMPLETE GUIDE

LIMESTONE AND SANDSTONE

Limestone is one of the most abundant sedimentary rocks. It is a medium-hard stone of fine, sandy appearance with occasional prominent grains or veins. It originates from various countries, including Portugal, Egypt, Italy, France, Israel, Spain and England. Lighter, paler colors are often used architecturally, but limestone occurs naturally in many different forms and colors, and is used in kitchens, bathrooms and for floors.

Properties: Like all natural stone, limestone has variations in structure, veining and tones; colors range from dark gray-black to speckled, golden, creamy or pinkish beige and near white. Nut brown and greenish grays also occur. Color and background are reasonably uniform. Types include: travertine (from Italy), with classic parallel veining in brown and tan; rosato, an even, pale pink; trani, beige pink; Ancaster mixed (from Lincolnshire, England), with wide tonal variation from blue to beige. Finishes can be polished to a reflective mirror gloss, honed (giving a satin smooth but nonreflective finish); riven or bush-hammered to give a rougher surface or tumbled (polished irregular shapes); it can also be sanded or aged. Limestone dissolves easily in acids (including vinegar), but is not sensitive to heat.

Use and Maintenance: Limestone floor and wall tiles are available in regular or random sizes for laying straight or diagonally, indoors or out. On patios or wet areas, a riven or textured surface can reduce slipping. Blocks can be cut to size for steps, stair treads and baseboards. Limestone is also used for countertops and backsplashes, basins, sinks, bathtubs and shower ledges, but its surface must be well protected and maintained. Surfaces should be sealed against chemical damage and staining. Sweep or vacuum clean. Wash when necessary with warm, soapy water.

Safety and Environment: This is a long-lasting, completely natural material. Its greatest environmental cost is in transportation, as it is often required far from where it naturally occurs.

Availability: From stone importers and suppliers, including tile and kitchen stores. Many specialized suppliers offer installation. Fireplace surrounds and artifacts are available through stonemasons and salvage and antique dealers.

Cost: ❹ High.

Specifications: Floor tiles: 12 or 16 in (305 or 400 mm) square, to 36 x 24 in (900 x 600 mm); ¾₀, ⅜ or ¾ in (10, 15 or 20 mm) thick. Counters: 25 or 36 in (625 or 900 mm) wide, 6½ or 10 ft (2 or 3 m) long.

GRANITE

Granite is a very hard stone with a coarse, granular but even-flecked pattern. From earliest times it was chosen as a principal building material and its legacy is visible across the world. Many colors occur, including beige and golden granite, pale rose, deep red; and browns, greens, blues, blacks and grays. Its surface can be polished to a mirror finish that is perfect for kitchen countertops.

Properties: Granite is a granular, crystalline rock, consisting of quartz, feldspar and mica in various combinations. Its more than 100 colors are due to varying feldspar content. It is one of the hardest, densest stones, with the aesthetic qualities of marble but much harder wearing. Its surface polishes well, but can also be shot-blasted, acid-washed, honed, riven, sanded, bush-hammered, tumbled, aged or thermally treated to fracture the crystals for a rough, skid-resistant texture. It is not sensitive to moderate to high heat.

Use and Maintenance: As granite can be polished to a very smooth finish, it makes a hygienic surface ideal for kitchen countertops and backsplashes — matching sinks and basins are also available. It is also fashioned into bathroom vanity units, lining for shower walls and floors, doorknobs, hearths and fireplace surrounds. Outdoors, its ability to withstand environmental effects makes it a good choice for garden paving, benches, fountains and features; it is also the traditional stone for Japanese garden lanterns and bridges. Its surface is porous and will stain if unsealed. Its extreme hardness means that most knives do not scratch it, but it will blunt knives, so use a cutting board on countertops. Chips can be repaired with matching granite dust mixed with epoxy resin.

Safety and Environment: Granite is a long-lasting, completely natural material. Its greatest environmental cost is in transportation, as it is often required far from where it naturally occurs.

Availability: From a wide range of stone importers and suppliers, including tile and kitchen stores. Many specialized suppliers offer installation. Fireplace surrounds and artifacts are available through stonemasons and salvage and antique dealers.

Cost: ❹ High.

Specifications: Floor tiles: 12 or 16 in (305 or 400 mm) square, to 36 x 24 in (900 x 600 mm); ⅜₀, ⅜ or ¾ in (10, 15 or 20 mm) thick. Counters can be cut to order (with sink openings, etc.).

MARBLE

Marble is a sparkling white form of limestone, known for the attractive veining that runs through and colors it. It is a delicately beautiful stone, easily worked, that has been used since ancient times for sculpture and building and still carries connotations of luxury and affluence. These qualities have made it widely sought after and, despite its weight and bulk, it has always been transported far from its origins.

Properties: Marble is a calcium carbonate stone, formed when calcium from shells and bones of prehistoric lifeforms combines with carbon dioxide from water. Pure calcite is white, and marble's veining is caused by mineral traces that vary from quarry to quarry: hematite adds red; limonite yellow; serpentine green; diopside blue. The best-known, carrara bianca (with gray veining), comes from Carrara, Italy. Marble is soft compared to granite and slate, and easily worked with sculptor's tools. Certain marbles are highly fragile due to irregular veining and may require liners or reinforcement. Marble crumbles readily when exposed to a moist atmosphere, and its surface will pit in rain unless properly sealed. It is heatproof, but can be stained and damaged by acids and must be sealed for high-traffic areas or kitchens.

Use and Maintenance: Marble has many suitable uses indoors, including fireplace surrounds, backsplashes and shower surrounds. Sinks, bowls, basins and bathtubs can be carved out of a single block. It is favored by cooks, but when used for countertops it must be sealed (reapply sealant every few years), and use cutting boards to avoid knife marks. Marble is easy to carve and highly tactile, so is a choice stone for carving into decorative features. Polished marble is slippery when wet, so not suitable as outdoor paving.

Safety and Environment: Marble is a long-lasting, completely natural material. Its greatest environmental cost is in transportation, as it is often required far from where it naturally occurs.

Availability: From a wide range of stone importers and suppliers, including tile and kitchen stores. Specialized suppliers offer installation. Fireplace surrounds and artifacts are available through stonemasons and salvage and antique dealers.

Cost: ❹ High.

Specifications: Floor tiles: 12 or 16 in (305 or 400 mm) square, to 36 x 24 in (900 x 600 mm); ⅜₀, ⅝ or ¾ in (10, 15 or 20 mm) thick. Counters can be cut to order (with sink openings, etc.).

WOOD • RUBBER, PLASTIC, RESIN & LINOLEUM • METAL • GLASS • FABRIC • PAPER • LEATHER • PAINT, VARNISH & LACQUER • **STONE, CERAMICS & TILES** • CONCRETE & CEMENT • PLASTER

INTERIOR MATERIALS & SURFACES: THE COMPLETE GUIDE

QUARRY TILES

QUARRY TILES

Quarry tiles are unglazed ceramic tiles with a rustic feel and appearance but a high level of performance. Traditionally, they were either a red terra-cotta color or dark gray-black, with a flat texture. Today tiles are produced in a variety of colors and textures, some of which mimic other products. They can be used in a variety of situations, both indoors and out.

Properties: Quarry tiles are made of natural clay fired at extremely high temperatures. They consist of the same hard-fired material all the way through and are highly durable. The characteristic brown-black "burn mark" across some tiles is created by flashing during firing. They have low moisture absorption, are frostproof and resistant to all acids except sulfuric. Tiles can be textured to resemble concrete, slate or wood grain. They are naturally nonslip, but some tiles are treaded with parallel lines across the surface to give even greater traction. Dark tile floors act as passive solar storage during the day, collecting heat that is then released slowly at night.

Use and Maintenance: These tiles are suitable for high-traffic areas and areas prone to moisture. Their nonslip quality makes them ideal for kitchens, utility rooms and around spas or pools. They can also be used as fireplace hearths or surrounds. Some have sharp, clean edges; others have irregular edges for a handmade appearance. As well as regular squares and oblongs, interlocking "sphinx" and "granada" shapes are also produced. Carreaux d'octagone have the corners cut off to accommodate small square inset tiles for pattern contrast. In areas of constant dampness or moisture, algae, mildew or mold may grow — a chemical sealant can reduce this. Sweep regularly and mop as necessary with soapy water.

Safety and Environment: Quarry tiles are made from natural materials without toxic additives and are safe to use, but some sealants are toxic. They are long-lasting and recyclable.

Availability: Tiles are available from building suppliers, flooring and floor tile shops, home-improvement retailers and salvage yards. Corresponding shaped nosing for steps and profiled strips for baseboards are also available.

Cost: ❸ Medium.

Specifications: 6 in (150 mm) square, but can be 2–12 in (50–300 mm) square; ¼, ½ or ⅝ in (6, 14 or 16 mm) thick. Interlocking: 5½ or 6½ in (135 or 165 mm) each way, ⅜ in (9 mm) thick.

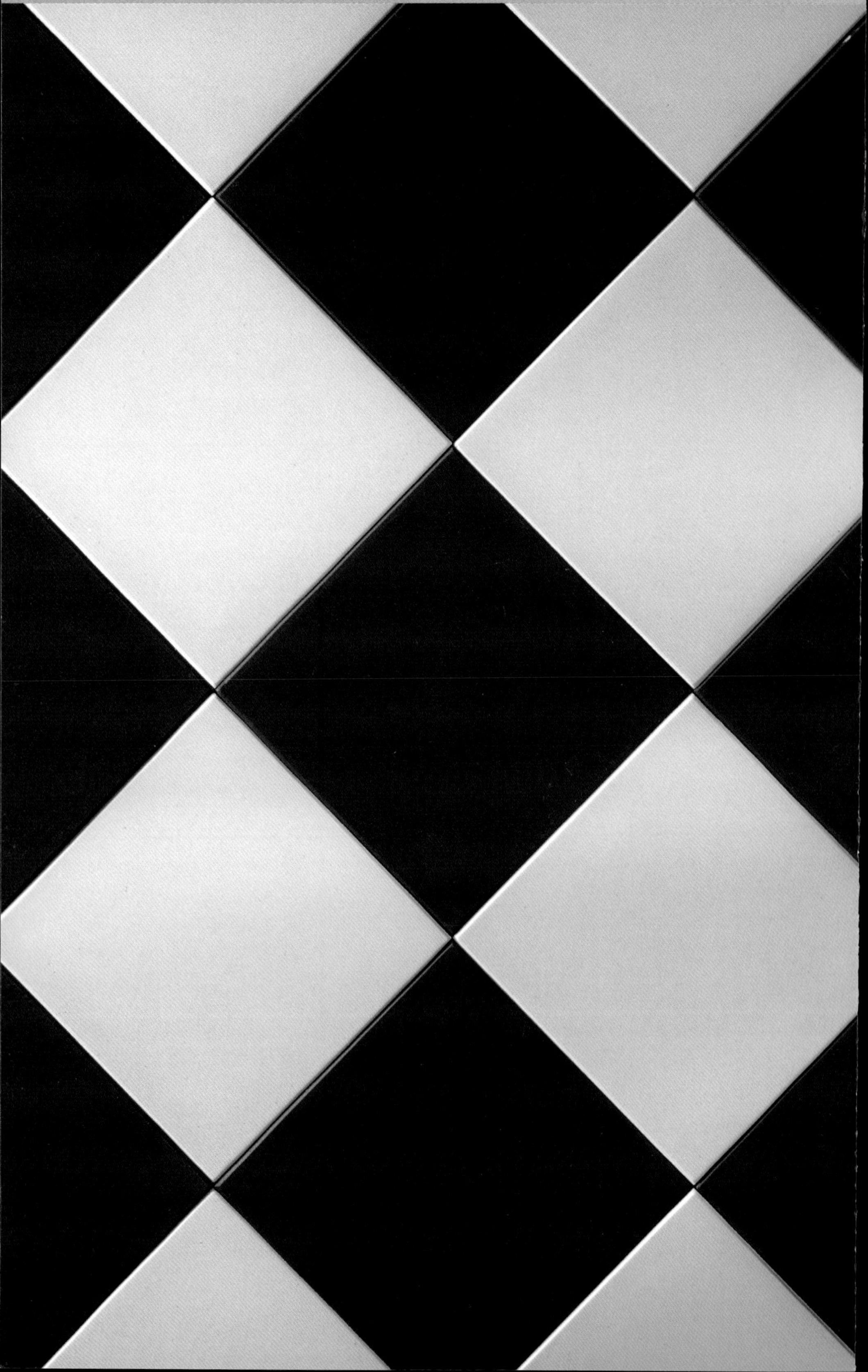

WOOD • RUBBER, PLASTIC, RESIN & LINOLEUM • METAL • GLASS • FABRIC • PAPER • LEATHER • PAINT, VARNISH & LACQUER • **STONE, CERAMICS & TILES** • CONCRETE & CEMENT • PLASTER

GEOMETRIC TILES

INTERIOR MATERIALS & SURFACES: THE COMPLETE GUIDE

GEOMETRIC TILES

Geometric and encaustic tiles are unglazed ceramic tiles used to create floor patterns. They were popular for entrance halls and front paths of English townhouses, mansion blocks and commercial premises from Victorian times to the 1930s, and known as tessellated floors since patterns were based on the marble mosaic floors of Italian churches. New tiles are available with the geometric patterns already laid out.

Properties: Plain-colored geometric tiles (usually black, white, terra-cotta, brown, blue or yellow) are formed into triangles, squares, trapeziums, hexagons and octagons, in modules that fit together to form complex patterns. Encaustic tiles are matching clay tiles, usually square, that have more complex patterns built up in layers of colored clay. Because these tiles are made of the same colored clay right through, their appearance does not change substantially with wear. They are highly durable, naturally nonslip and have low moisture absorption. They are also frostproof and resist all acids except sulfuric.

Use and Maintenance: They are mainly produced today for restoration and repair of old geometric floors. Many colors, sizes and patterns can be made to order. Some new tile modules (with preset patterns) are black and white only; others use the full color range. Border patterns are available to edge the pattern's perimeter. Tiles are usually laid with adhesive and have very fine grout lines. When creating a new geometric tile floor, it should be set on a concrete or plywood subfloor. Interior tiled floors should be sealed with specific sealants once adhesive and grout have cured. Exterior floors should not be sealed. As long as tiles are firmly installed, they are suitable for areas of heavy traffic, indoors or out.

Safety and Environment: These tiles are made from natural materials without the use of toxic additives, so are safe to use. Some sealants are toxic, however. Tiles are long-lasting and recyclable.

Availability: From salvage yards, building suppliers, flooring and floor tile stores and some home-improvement retailers.

Cost: ❸ Medium.

Specifications: 1½–6 in (38–150 mm) square; right-angled, equilateral triangles; rectangles: 1–6 x 3 in (25–150 x 75 mm); also hexagons, octagons, half-octagons or trapeziums.

WOOD • RUBBER, PLASTIC, RESIN & LINOLEUM • METAL • GLASS • FABRIC • PAPER • LEATHER • PAINT, VARNISH & LACQUER • **STONE, CERAMICS & TILES** • CONCRETE & CEMENT • PLASTER

CERAMIC TILES

INTERIOR MATERIALS & SURFACES: THE COMPLETE GUIDE

CERAMIC TILES

Originally, wall and floor tiles were marble and other fine stones cut into simple or complex patterns to provide a hard-wearing decorative surface. These were replaced by more affordable glazed ceramic tiles. Today there is an endless selection of colors, textures and patterns, with new materials incorporated all the time (glass, metal and natural stone). Spanish manufacturers produce most of today's premier ceramic tiles.

Properties: Ceramic tiles are made of clay, silica, fluxes, colorings and other raw materials, and given an impermeable, vitreous enamel surface. The unglazed backs of wall tiles are more porous than floor tiles, to aid adhesion. Glazes are generally tough; certain dark, pigment-rich colors can be less so. Tiles can be flat or embossed with a pattern. Ceramic tiles are hard-wearing, easy to clean, stain- and heat-resistant, waterproof and inflammable.

Use and Maintenance: Ceramic tiles provide a functional, hygienic covering for walls, floors and other surfaces. They can be used externally for facing walls or on windowsills and for decorative fireplace surrounds or tabletops. Tiny tiles for creating a mosaic effect come attached in sets on paper or mesh backing sheets for quicker laying. Most glazed tiles are waterproof, but even waterproof grouts can let through small leaks, so, where necessary, apply tiles to a waterproof surface (cement board or waterproof composite boards).

For countertops, use smooth grout or apply sealant to preserve color and maintain hygiene. Use anti-mildew grout sealant in damp areas such as showers. Floor tiles generally comprise harder, thicker clay than wall tiles, with low porosity and water absorption, and a more durable surface. Although floor tiles can be applied to walls, wall tiles should not be used on floors or work surfaces.

Safety and Environment: Ceramic tiles are manu-factured using the same natural materials and firing methods employed for centuries. They are stable and safe to use and live with. Tiles are reusable. They will not biodegrade, but neither are they toxic.

Availability: From tile stores, building suppliers and home-improvement retailers. Available in numerous colors in gloss, satin or crackle glaze finishes.

Cost: ❸ Medium.

Specifications: Square, oblong, hexagon, regular or irregular shapes from ½ in (12 mm) square (mosaic) to 12 x 12 in (300 x 300 mm). Contrasting or coordinating strips available to match.

WOOD • RUBBER, PLASTIC, RESIN & LINOLEUM • METAL • GLASS • FABRIC • PAPER • LEATHER • PAINT, VARNISH & LACQUER • STONE, CERAMICS & TILES • CONCRETE & CEMENT • PLASTER

HANDMADE WALL TILES

INTERIOR MATERIALS & SURFACES: THE COMPLETE GUIDE

HANDMADE WALL TILES

Handmade and hand-painted tiles are produced by processes similar to those used in mass production, but batches are smaller and tiles can be made to order. Hand-produced tiles are valued for their rustic textures or the artistry of the patterns. Tiles can be individually decorated or painted in a series to form a large pattern or scene. Handmade tiles are entirely hand-formed, from terra-cotta or white-bodied clay.

Properties: Hand-painting is usually done on preglazed commercial tiles, then overfired with a ceramic glaze (often weaker than vitreous enamel). Hand-formed tiles, in standard or special sizes, are commonly thicker than mass-produced tiles, with a variable edge. They can be flat or with a bas relief or pressed pattern. Cuerda seca replicates the complex geometric or floral designs from the Moorish and Spanish tiling tradition. Wall tiles are usually glazed with wipeable finishes, but require care around fragile projecting areas. Glazes are generally tough, but some dark colors are more fragile. Tiles are long-lasting, durable, stain- and heat-resistant, waterproof and inflammable.

Use and Maintenance: Handmade tiles can be used as functional surfaces such as backsplashes or shower enclosures or used as a decorative panel or frieze. Most are suitable outdoors. Tiles for countertops or power showers require high-quality glaze. Tiles can be adhered to walls or treated like a picture and hung with or without a mount or frame. They may also be incorporated into frames or table-tops. Embossed and overpainted tiles are intended for walls; some flatter types are suitable for floors — it is unwise to use wall tiles on floors or countertops. Use wider grout lines with rustic or irregular-edged tiles. Seal grout if susceptible to staining or bacteria. Apply tiles to a waterproof surface if waterproofing is essential.

Safety and Environment: Ceramic tiles are stable and safe to use and live with. They are reusable. They will not biodegrade, but neither are they toxic.

Availability: From tile stores and direct from artists (who will take commissions).

Cost: ❹ High.

Specifications: Usually square or oblong, typically 6 x 6 or 4 x 8 in (150 x 150 or 100 x 200 mm) to coordinate with standard sizes. Some artisans produce complementing borders or decorative strips.

SALVAGED TILES

Ceramic tiles and enamel-faced bricks were once common features of old train stations, hospitals, schools, kitchens, hotels and stores such as butcher shops. They have been stripped out of a great number of buildings during modernization and many — especially highly decorative Victorian tiles — are now available through architectural salvage dealers and in demand for incorporating into homes today.

Properties: The process of removing tiles for reuse is costly and highly skilled. Salvaged tiles must be thoroughly cleaned and prepared by specialized conservators. The glaze of some may be pitted or cracked, requiring restoration. Tile quantities vary widely. Choice may range from identical, plain tiles with a complementary border to multi-tile panels that make up a large scene or signage. Tiles are usually glazed to a high-gloss finish. When properly installed, salvaged tiles have the same hygienic, durable, heat-resistant, waterproof and inflammable properties as their modern equivalents.

Use and Maintenance: Installation methods have changed since Victorian times and salvaged tiles do not look right if fitted using modern techniques (grout lines, for instance, must be thinner and extremely tidy). A craftsperson skilled in conservation tilework should be hired to lay them. They can be used in areas susceptible to moderate amounts of heat and moisture: kitchens, bathrooms, living or dining rooms. Commonly available tiles are those for insetting into the sides of fireplace surrounds and for wainscot areas in hallways. Tiles can be set directly onto the wall's surface or onto a prepared surface such as a lumber panel or a wooden frame. Salvaged tiles should not be used on floors unless it is known they are suitable for this purpose.

Safety and Environment: The rising cash value of salvaged Victorian tiles is prompting an increase in theft from buildings. Tile conservation associations should be able to confirm whether or not a tile job lot was legitimate salvage.

Availability: Through antique dealers, salvage yards and auctions. Some tile suppliers may also stock or be able to supply.

Cost: ❹ High.

Specifications: Usually available in standard imperial dimensions, typically 6 x 6, 2 x 6 or 4 x 8 in (150 x 150, 50 x 150 or 100 x 200 mm) with corresponding borders 2 or 3 in (50 or 75 mm) wide.

GLASS TILES

Glass tiles draw on traditional techniques of glass artists, jewelry-making and ceramic-tile manufacture to form brilliantly colored tiles that can be used on walls for a dramatic yet practical surface. As well as regular-sized glass tiles, mosaic patterns of tiny glass tiles or tesserae are produced for a range of creative designs. Glass tiles are particularly effective where their translucence and sparkle can be appreciated.

Properties: Tiles can be pure glass or a combination of glass and ceramic, some with mixed or contrasting colors, others with metallic finishes. They can be produced by fusing — joining colored glass pieces by melting at high temperatures — and slumping (see page 99). Slumped glass tiles often vary in depth and feature tiny bubbles. These diffuse the light and distort images, reducing transparency but creating interesting effects. Glass tiles are scratch-resistant, durable, hygienic, frostproof and inflammable. They are impervious to water and staining, and resist chemical attack.

Use and Maintenance: Glass tiles perform well in areas of high moisture. They work well outdoors where brilliant colors are highlighted by the sun; they can also be incorporated into stained-glass windows. Most are not suitable for floors, because they are slippery when wet. Many tiles have a raised decorative effect. Flat tiles are extremely hard, making ideal countertops. Most are translucent, so any coloring or patterning on the underlying surface needs to be considered; adhesive also needs careful application to avoid marring the finished effect. Glass mosaic tiles are attached in sets to paper or mesh backing sheets for quicker laying; they can be used alone (ready-made designs are available) or in conjunction with ceramic tiles. Install with standard tiling tools. Clean with glass cleaners. Protect highly textured areas from dried-on dirt.

Safety and Environment: Glass products are recyclable, and glass tiles occasionally make use of recycled glass.

Availability: From glass craft outlets, tile stores and home-improvement retailers. Special tiles can be made to order or produced as artwork.

Cost: ❹ High.

Specifications: Match ceramic tiles dimensions (see page 205) for use together; contrasting strips ½–1 x 8 in (12–25 x 200 mm), about ¼ in (4–6 mm) thick.

STAMPED TILES

Using stamps to transfer a design onto tiles achieves an exactly replicated pattern on each tile. The technique is used both in mechanized tile manufacture and on handmade tiles. Many traditional patterns are delicate, complex drawings transferred onto tiles in one or more colors. Stamped tiles are usually ornately patterned and often appear as feature tiles in a larger expanse of more simply decorated tiles.

Properties: Stamped designs can be applied with high-tech machinery or by hand (rubber stamps). Stamps can be used alone or in conjunction with other painting or coloring techniques. All stamped tiles have a flat surface, and the stamps are usually printed over a primary glaze. Tile style, size and edges can vary. Stamped tiles have a clear finish to preserve and protect their pattern. They maintain the characteristics of all ceramic glazed tiles: long-lasting, durable, stain- and heat-resistant, waterproof and inflammable.

Use and Maintenance: Stamped tiles can transform a room with a new texture or motif, bringing new life to an existing tiled area or adding color and interest to bland tiles. Stamping features on both floor and wall tiles, and their protective finish makes them suitable for heavily trafficked and moist environments, including kitchen and bathroom walls or backsplashes, fireplace surrounds, hearths or windowsills. Certain antique or fragile tiles require a protected position. Feature tiles can be mounted and used as wall hangings or trivets. Existing ceramic tiles can also be stamped (new or in place): clean thoroughly and prepare with tile-priming paint (a colored matte overcoat may also be required). They can then be stamped or stenciled by hand, touching up or highlighting designs with additional painting. Apply a minimum of three coats of clear acrylic urethane as a protective seal.

Safety and Environment: Stamped tiles are stable, safe to use and live with and are reusable. They will not biodegrade, but neither are they toxic.

Availability: From tile stores, building suppliers and home-improvement retailers; antique and architectural salvage dealers. Numerous colors and patterns are available, with a gloss, satin or crackle glaze finish.

Cost: ❸–❹ Medium to high.

Specifications: In standard sizes, usually 4, 5 or 6 in (100, 125 or 150 mm) square.

BRICKS

Brickwork has a warm, reassuring, tactile character arising from the bricks' natural material and color. Modern bricks are mass-produced in molds or by extruding the clay through a brick-sized die and wire-cutting to size, but are essentially the same material used for centuries. Despite increased standardization, some regions are still characterized by particular shades of brick color and styles of bricklaying.

Properties: Color and texture vary according to the clay (terra-cotta, cream, black, brown, blue), fuel and firing temperature, and any additions, such as carbons, salt, pebbles or glass. Bricks can be glazed with colored enamels. Bricks are effective insulators, retaining indoor heat in winter and keeping cool in summer. They also "breathe," accommodating atmospheric changes. They are a solid material with high compressive strength, and are naturally fire-resistant. Some clay is relatively soft; other brick faces deteriorate due to age or pollution (prevent by using chemical sealant). Bricks are baked at high temperatures to withstand harsh weather. Their regular size facilitates handling and flexible use.

Use and Maintenance: Bricks are a common building material, used structurally or as weatherproof facing. A brick wall is laid in courses, combining stretchers (long side facing out) and headers (short side out) to form patterns or bonds — the standard pattern of alternating stretchers and headers is called a running bond. Common bond has five rows of stretchers, then a row of headers. English, Flemish and herringbone are other common bonds. Bricks are also suitable for patios, driveways and paths. Correctly installed, brickwork is maintenance-free. Efflorescence (a white, powdery salt deposit) can be removed with chemical treatment. Antique or salvaged bricks sawed into strips ½ inch (1.25 cm) thick make an alternative to ceramic floor tiles.

Safety and Environment: Bricks are made from natural clay.

Availability: From building suppliers.

Cost: ❸ Medium.

Specifications: Standard bricks: 8½ x 4 x 2¾ in (215 x 102 x 70 mm). Old salvaged brick and those of foreign origin vary. Special shapes are available for creating arches, curves and decorative details.

WOOD • RUBBER, PLASTIC, RESIN & LINOLEUM • METAL • GLASS • FABRIC • PAPER • LEATHER • PAINT, VARNISH & LACQUER • STONE, CERAMICS & TILES • CONCRETE & CEMENT • PLASTER

SLATE

INTERIOR MATERIALS & SURFACES: THE COMPLETE GUIDE

SLATE

Unlike the dense, solid form of most rock, slate splits easily into thin sheets. Because of this it is widely used for roofing and siding, but it also makes practical and attractive kitchen and bathroom countertops. About 60 natural colors occur, from black and deep gray to greens and reddish browns; coloring can be flat and highly uniform or show quite marked variegation.

Properties: Slate is fireproof and unaffected by the sun. It does not support moss or fungal growth (even in damp, shady areas), and is nonporous and water-repellant. Slate resists acids and pollutants. It is moderately insulating from heat and cold; dark colors absorb and store heat, releasing it slowly. Slate has a naturally riven finish, providing a nonslip surface. In certain Welsh quarries, slate is processed into roofing tiles directly as it is mined.

Use and Maintenance: This stone is suitable for high-traffic areas and can be exposed to the atmosphere without using a surface sealant. On floors it will act as passive solar storage during the day, releasing it slowly at night. Slate is used for fireplace hearths and surrounds. Slate tiles can be used exposing their smooth cut face or stacked to form a feature of the rough edges — an effect that works well for retaining walls, window arches and step risers. Slate makes smooth, practical countertops and backsplashes when highly

polished or oiled; reapply oil whenever the finish looks dull. It is used in bathrooms for vanity units, basins, shower floors and surrounds. As well as roof tiles and wall cladding, other outdoor uses include paving for paths and patios, retaining and facing walls, pool or spa surrounds, landscaping and water features.

Safety and Environment: This is a long-lasting, completely natural material. Its greatest environmental cost is in transportation, as it is often required far from where it naturally occurs.

Availability: From a wide range of stone importers and suppliers, floor tile and kitchen stores, building suppliers and home-improvement retailers. Many specialized suppliers offer installation.

Cost: ❸ Medium.

Specifications: Roofing slate in standard sizes. Floor tiles: 12 or 16 in (305 or 400 mm) square, to 36 x 24 in (900 x 600 mm); ⅗₀, ⅜ or ¾ in (10, 15 or 20 mm) thick. Countertops can be cut and detailed to order.

217

CONCRETE & CEMENT

Concrete is made from a mixture of gritty aggregate, water and cement (a fine powder of limestone and clay). Together with the water, the cement acts as a bonding agent to set the materials. Concrete is thought of as a modern material, but was used in ancient times in a form not so very different from what we know today. The Assyrians and Babylonians made concrete with clay as the cement agent, and the Egyptians used lime and gypsum in their concrete. The Romans used crushed volcanic rock pozzolan cement in the construction of the Appian Way, the Colosseum and the Roman baths.

Modern cement was developed in England in the 18th century, with crushed brick added as a strengthener. The recipe was improved in 1824 when limestone and clay were burned together, changing the chemical properties of the materials and further strengthening it to create Portland cement, which is still commonly used today. Additives have been added to cement to alter or create properties such as curing time, strength of hardening and water or fire resistance. Structural poured concrete, as used in major construction work, uses coarse gravel, but very fine aggregate, such as sand, can be used for a smooth finish.

Concrete reinforced with wire mesh or bars combines the compressive strength of the concrete with the tensile strength of the embedded metal to prevent cracking. Developments in reinforced concrete have allowed for increasingly creative and

abstract structures to be constructed, from skyscrapers and bridges to safe homes in earthquake or hurricane zones.

Many building components are made from precast concrete, including bricks and blocks, floor and ceiling slabs, paving slabs and culverts. These come in a variety of standard sizes, but pigments can be added to change the color, and various alternative materials added to the aggregate, such as marble or salvaged metal, can give the final product a very different character. The surface can also be molded or pitted, hammered, or washed to create interesting surface textures and effects. Concrete can also be used as a surface treatment to provide a waterproof or textured surface coating for floors or the inside or outside of walls, and its appearance enhanced by many of the means used for precast items.

In addition to being formed into precast components or applied as a surface coating, concrete can be cast on site. For this, a form or mold, known as shuttering, is built in place, usually using an inexpensive sheet lumber such as plywood. The concrete is then poured in and left to cure before the shuttering is removed. This technique is commonly used for footings, foundations, floors and footpaths, but can also be applied to the construction of kitchen countertops and even bathtubs.

WOOD • RUBBER, PLASTIC, RESIN & LINOLEUM • METAL • GLASS • FABRIC • PAPER • LEATHER • PAINT, VARNISH & LACQUER • STONE, CERAMICS & TILES • **CONCRETE & CEMENT** • PLASTER

CONCRETE SLABS

INTERIOR MATERIALS & SURFACES: THE COMPLETE GUIDE

CONCRETE SLABS

Concrete is cast in slabs, either on site or in precast modules to make drying, handling and transportation easier. Slabs can be rough or smooth, natural or colored, and, in addition to providing a utility material for paving and subfloors, can be a feature in their own right, especially if various materials such as glass, nuts and bolts or microchips are added to the mix for visual interest.

Properties: Additives can increase concrete's strength, waterproofing, frost resistance or drying time. Pigments and decorative aggregates are added for color or a quality finish. Concrete can be colored by staining (acid etching) with metallic and mineral salts combined with color compounds in a water-based solution. Concrete is highly impact-resistant, strong in compression and stain-resistant if polished and sealed. Sheering and tension vary depending on concrete constituents. Concrete is brittle in freezing conditions, and wind- and fire-resistant, although extremely high temperatures can cause damage.

Use and Maintenance: Basic slabs are cast on site or precast for floor and roof deck, or subfloor paving. Slabs for patios or driveways can be ordered in natural concrete or stone look. Floors can be cast, polished, scored and stained to resemble stone slab floors. Polishing with progressively finer and finer grinders will smooth and burnish the surface. Precast concrete bathtubs, basins and sinks are available; these are heavy, so check floor structure before installing. Floor paints (see page 177) generate a bright, basic finish, or sophisticated paint effects can mimic marble or tiles (finish with urethane topcoat). Other uses include vandalproof outdoor furniture, stylish indoor furniture, kitchen counters (polished to a stain-resistant, hygienic surface), fireplace surrounds and hearths. Use fireproof concrete to line fireplaces.

Safety and Environment: Concrete is made from natural materials and is nontoxic, although chemical additives may be potentially toxic. It will not break down, but can be broken up and recycled as hardcore and aggregate.

Availability: From building suppliers and home-improvement retailers for raw materials or components, and specialized contractors for customized items.

Cost: ❷–❹ Low to high.

Specifications: Available as precast components such as windowsills, steps and outdoor paving slabs; bathroom or living room furniture and customized items (floors, countertops).

WOOD • RUBBER, PLASTIC, RESIN & LINOLEUM • METAL • GLASS • FABRIC • PAPER • LEATHER • PAINT, VARNISH & LACQUER • STONE, CERAMICS & TILES • **CONCRETE & CEMENT** • PLASTER

ROUGH AND RENDERED CONCRETE

INTERIOR MATERIALS & SURFACES: THE COMPLETE GUIDE

ROUGH AND RENDERED CONCRETE

Most concrete surfaces need to be treated with a finishing layer. This is commonly cement render, applied to the surface of structural concrete to improve weather-proofing outside or as a barrier to moisture below ground level inside. Whether needed for protection or not, cement render can also be used to create a smooth, aesthetically pleasing surface finish or a decorative texture such as pebbledash.

Properties: Renders — surface coats of cement applied for a smooth or textured finish — are made of similar materials to concrete (sand, cement and aggregate), but mixed to a consistency liquid enough to apply with a sprayer or trowel, yet stiff enough to adhere to a vertical surface. Additives can create frostproof or waterproof render. Various aggregates or pigments can be added for attractive finishes. The surface of the base material must be porous or rough so the cement render can adhere. Renders are resistant to impact damage, wind and fire, although extremely high temperatures may cause damage.

Use and Maintenance: Internal or external waterproof render is used to create a waterproof seal on concrete walls in basements or lower ground floors. External cement render containing fine sand or pigments can double as a weatherproof coating and a decorative finish. It can either be smoothed flat for a paintable surface or textured with the addition of aggregate. This pebbled surface can be painted or can include pigment or exotic aggregates in the mix to achieve a maintenance-free decorative finish. Render must be applied to a sufficient depth — usually not less than ½ inch (1.25 cm) — to ensure adequate strength. Cracks must be repaired immediately or penetrating moisture will cause chunks to fall off.

Safety and Environment: Render is made from natural materials and is nontoxic, although chemical additives may be potentially toxic. It will not break down, but can be broken up and recycled as hardcore and aggregate.

Availability: Building suppliers and home-improvement retailers stock raw materials.

Cost: ❸ Medium.

Specifications: Available as powder cement to mix with water and aggregate.

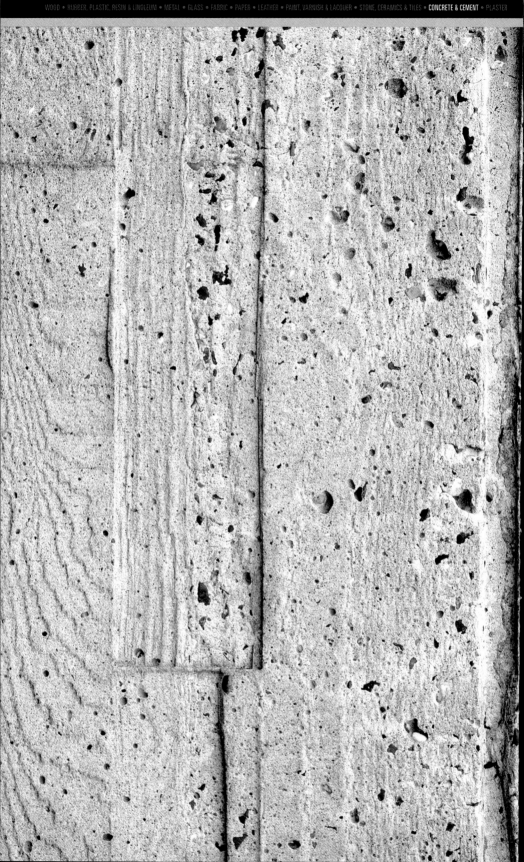

SHATTERED CEMENT AND CONCRETE

Concrete blocks are either molded or extruded, and have a bland, regular surface. The appearance of both blocks and poured concrete can be enhanced in a number of ways. The underlying aggregates in cast surfaces can be revealed by sandblasting, and a tooled cement surface over poured concrete can conceal what would otherwise show the imprint of the lumber shuttering used to form the concrete mold.

Properties: Sandblasting the top layer provides a riven, shattered look, exposing the concrete's inner components. A similar effect is achieved by applying a temporary surface to the new cement (to prevent drying), then wire brushing. Decorative facing blocks with a riven, shattered surface expose a natural, sandy finish. They often include colored pigment (dark/light gray, cream, ocher, brown, tan, terra-cotta, slate blue). Cast surfaces can be disguised or transformed by tooling: a thin layer of cement render is applied to the concrete, then textured or stamped with a pattern to mimic natural stone or brickwork. Concrete finishes are hard-wearing, but susceptible to staining unless sealed.

Use and Maintenance: Shattered facing blocks are weatherproof and usually intended for external use. They can be used alone, in combinations of different colors or with stone for a heavily textured, rusticated effect. Exposed aggregate offers a stable, pebbled finish that is slightly irregular and therefore nonslip. It is beautiful outdoors, especially as paving around swimming pools and in areas of heavy traffic, but should not be subject to grease and grime. Tooled patterns can be cut into new colored cement render with a stencil or engraved into existing concrete, to change the appearance of patios, driveways or paths. Shattered and tooled finishes are suitable for walls indoors and out where a heavy-duty rustic surface is required.

Safety and Environment: Concrete can be recycled as hardcore and aggregate.

Availability: From building suppliers and some home-improvement retailers; stencils for imprinting patterns are available from the same source.

Cost: ❸ Medium.

Specifications: Concrete blocks in about 18 standard sizes. Commonly: 16 x 8 x 4 in (400 x 200 x 100 mm). Most sizes and shape of natural stone or gravel aggregate are available for casting in concrete.

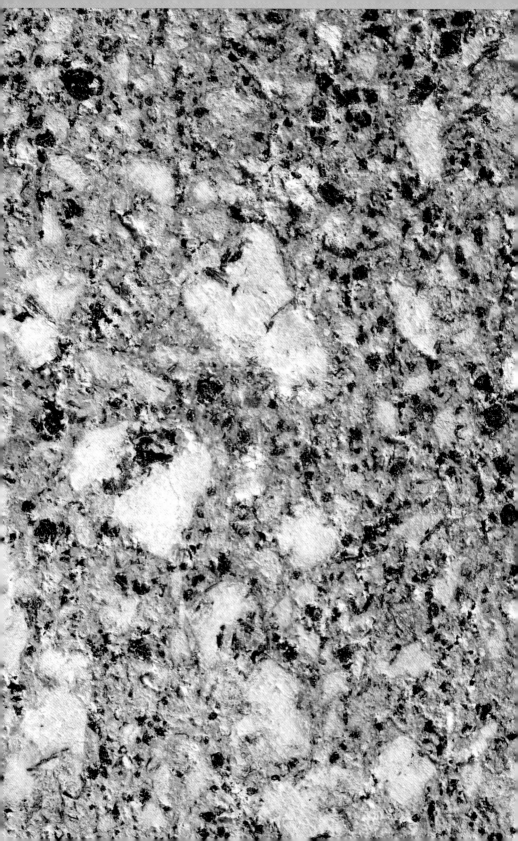

TERRAZZO

 Terrazzo is a composite, stone-based material in which chips of marble, quartz, granite or glass bound in the basic cement and/or resin mix give sparkle and interest. Terrazzo is either precast or poured on site in sections, and polished to a smooth, even texture to expose the stone aggregates. It is suitable for outdoor and indoor use and provides a durable, low-maintenance floor in areas of heavy traffic.

Properties: Types are standard, Venetian or palladiana (depending on aggregate size and mixture), or categorized by texture (e.g., rustic terrazzo). Additives create grades resistant to chemicals, acids or alkalis, and terrazzo suitable for damp areas or for laying extremely thinly. To avoid cracking when drying, expansion strips are necessary; these can be brass, zinc or colored plastic and must be factored into a pattern. Terrazzo can be hand-formed into molding edges (a practical alternative to baseboard) or features such as stair nosings. Terrazzo is not waterproof, but can be sealed with a slip-resistant sealant. It is heavier and thicker than most flooring, and is porous, so absorbs oils and will discolor if unsealed.

Use and Maintenance: Terrazzo must be applied to a stable concrete subfloor. It is cast in small individual sections (usually 1 sq yd/m² or less) between dividing strips. Exact aggregate and cement colors can be selected when ordering — a sample is then made up. Terrazzo is suitable for all floors and some walls. If well sealed, it can be used for kitchen counters and backsplashes. For bathroom floors or shower ledges, additional waterproofing must be incorporated in the subfloor. Terrazzo features in many precast items, such as steps, benches and planters. Clean with neutral cleaners (not all-purpose cleaners). Wipe up spills immediately. Keep swept, as grit may scratch.

Safety and Environment: Terrazzo is a safe, nontoxic material that makes use of very small chips of stone that would otherwise be a waste product. It is not recycled.

Availability: Available from specialized marble and flooring suppliers.

Cost: ❹ High.

Specifications: Laid in various thicknesses ¼–1 in (6–25 mm) with additional built-up areas such as baseboards.

WOOD • RUBBER, PLASTIC, RESIN & LINOLEUM • METAL • GLASS • FABRIC • PAPER • LEATHER • PAINT, VARNISH & LACQUER • STONE, CERAMICS & TILES • **CONCRETE & CEMENT** • PLASTER

CONCRETE BLOCKS

INTERIOR MATERIALS & SURFACES: THE COMPLETE GUIDE

CONCRETE BLOCKS

 Concrete blocks are a cost-effective, easy-to-use building component, produced in a variety of different forms. They are used predominantly for utilitarian structural work, such as walls and screens, but come in a variety of sizes and shapes that can also be used decoratively, indoors as well as outdoors. Blocks can be plastered, painted or sealed with transparent matte sealants to expose their original texture and color.

Properties: Blocks are cast or extruded into concrete components developed to incorporate many different properties. Structural concrete blocks are a heavyweight material designed to withstand substantial compressive forces. All blocks are noncombustible, but some have additional fire-resistant properties, reducing heat transmission and improving structural ability. Some have a high insulation value; others feature an acoustic sound-reduction component (these are often lightweight). Hollow-core blocks provide a natural barrier against moisture, minimizing condensation transmission across the block. Exact, regular dimensions, in a broad modular range of shapes and sizes, and sharp, even edges make concrete blocks an easy material to work with. Most require a waterproofing sealant or a layer of concrete mixture to the outside.

Use and Maintenance: Blocks are suitable for outdoor or indoor use, and although most need sealing to weatherproof, the majority retain their integrity and characteristics in damp conditions. Blocks are designed to form dividing or structural walls or screens, and can also be used to construct outdoor furniture or barbecues. Those intended for garden retaining walls are formed with a cavity designed to be filled with soil and act as a small planter. Large expanses of concrete are prone to graffiti, so various environmentally friendly products have been developed for removing paint and other stains from concrete blocks.

Safety and Environment: Concrete blocks are safe and easy to use and can be recycled as hardcore or aggregate.

Availability: Stocked by building suppliers and a limited range by home-improvement retailers.

Cost: ❷ Low.

Specifications: In about 18 standard sizes. Commonly: 16 x 8 x 4 in (400 x 200 x 100 mm). Curved blocks, corners and 45-degree angles are also available, as well as sills, curbs and channels.

WOOD • RUBBER, PLASTIC, RESIN & LINOLEUM • METAL • GLASS • FABRIC • PAPER • LEATHER • PAINT, VARNISH & LACQUER • STONE, CERAMICS & TILES • **CONCRETE & CEMENT** • PLASTER

FLAGSTONE PAVING

INTERIOR MATERIALS & SURFACES: THE COMPLETE GUIDE

FLAGSTONE PAVING

Flagstone paving is an Edwardian technique of laying irregular, naturally shaped stone or slate pavers. The stones are arranged in a pattern reminiscent of cracking on old glazes. The technique can also utilize specially shaped concrete paving stones or broken pavers. Flagstone paving is more expensive to lay than regular shapes due to the level of skill required for a good finish.

Properties: Irregular stones can be arranged in various ways, so it is important to lay them out before adhering. Precast flags in irregular shapes are specially made for the job. Broken up rectangular paving slabs can be used, but the numerous right angles must be trimmed or worked into the design. Precast concrete paving slabs are usually colorfast and frost-resistant. They are easy to maintain and, with appropriate bedding, are hard-wearing and suitable for areas of heavy and vehicular traffic.

Use and Maintenance: Flagstone paving can be used anywhere that regular paving would be used: for floors, patios and pathways. Use nonslip concrete paving around pools. Unlike regular paving slabs (which can be laid on sand), it is advisable to lay flagstones on concrete a minimum of 2 inches (5 cm) thick; for a driveway, use heavy-duty concrete bedding at least 4 inches (10 cm) thick. Flagstone paving can be random or accommodate a pattern of regular contrasting pavers or terra-cotta tiles to

achieve a geometric design. The relative expense in laying an irregular pattern is due to the time required to achieve a tight, uniform jigsaw and the extensive, irregular grouting to the mortar joints. The skill of flagstone paving is in arranging the stones so that the mortar joint is minimized — large joints fail within a few years.

Safety and Environment: Concrete paving stones are safe and easy to use and can be recycled as hardcore or aggregate.

Availability: From garden centers, building suppliers, home-improvement retailers and salvage dealers.

Cost: ❷ Low.

Specifications: Irregular shaped paving slabs are available in natural stone and slate as well as precast concrete slabs: thicknesses from 1–3 in (25–75 mm).

WOOD • RUBBER, PLASTIC, RESIN & LINOLEUM • METAL • GLASS • FABRIC • PAPER • LEATHER • PAINT, VARNISH & LACQUER • STONE, CERAMICS & TILES • **CONCRETE & CEMENT** • PLASTER

CONCRETE AND STRAW

INTERIOR MATERIALS & SURFACES: THE COMPLETE GUIDE

CONCRETE AND STRAW

Building from straw is an ancient technique that has been recently revived by those interested in sustainable, ecological building techniques. The compressed structure and thermal insulation of stacked straw bales combines with the weather- and fire-proofing achieved by a concrete render to create a viable alternative building technology. Straw decomposes very slowly and it will not deteriorate if kept dry.

Properties: The foundation of concrete and straw buildings is usually a layer of concrete heavily insulated underneath. A load-bearing straw bale system of walls is built upon this, in an interlocking pattern, like brickwork, strengthened with steel or bamboo reinforcing rods or lumber posts and beams. Wire mesh wrapped around the straw provides a tooth for the cement render. Although straw is normally highly flammable, when packed densely for structural and thermal purposes, the lack of oxygen reduces its flammability and it can burn more slowly than lumber (but it will still burn at very high temperatures). The greatest danger is mildew, which attacks wet straw.

Use and Maintenance: Most straw and concrete projects are residential, one-story and experimental, but the technology is spreading and developing, especially in areas where high-tech materials are unavailable or unaffordable. It not only produces low-cost, well-insulated buildings, but also utilizes raw materials that are produced without great damage to the environment — straw is a natural by-product of the food industry, does not break down for composting and is produced in surplus quantities. Given knowledgeable management, most concrete and straw projects can be built with hand tools and unskilled labor. Maintenance depends on the quality of the render; a sophisticated professional application will be more expensive initially, but should last longer with less upkeep.

Safety and Environment: Entirely safe and environmentally sustainable. However, if straw bales are not available locally, transporting them reduces the environmental effectiveness of the product. There is also a danger of moisture damage in transit.

Availability: Source straw bales from a nearby rural community. They must be produced to the requisite size and density for building.

Cost: ❷ Low.

Specifications: Usual dimensions: 14 x 30 x 39 in (350 x 750 x 1,000 mm) or 16 x 24 x 48 in (400 x 600 x 1,200 mm). Half-bales will be required to make up the staggered pattern.

RENDERED AND CUT

Many structural concrete surfaces need to be treated with a finishing layer of cement render to make them weatherproof. Applying this finishing surface also offers the opportunity to incorporate patterns and textures into the render, creating the effect of other materials, such as stone or tiles. These patterns can be stamped into the surface when it is still wet or cut into it when dry.

Properties: Cement renders can be stamped, cut or sawed to create alternative textures. Renders must have a consistency liquid enough to hand-work, but stiff enough so they adhere to a vertical surface, and the surface below must be porous or rough enough for render to adhere. Additives are used to make render frost- or water-proof. Renders are resistant to impact damage, wind and fire, although extremely high temperatures may cause damage.

Use and Maintenance: External render can be both a weatherproof coating and a decorative finish. In addition to being left flat to provide a smooth, paintable surface or textured (see page 223), cement render can be imprinted with patterns. Stencils suitable for use on render are available for imprinting a variety of authentic patterns, including cobbles, tiles, tooled (cut) stone or rough-shaped field stones. Render must be applied to a sufficient depth, usually not less than ½ inch (1.25 cm), to ensure adequate strength. Cracks must be repaired immediately or penetrating moisture will cause chunks to fall off. As an alternative to creating patterns in the wet render, cured concrete surfaces can be cut using power tools to create brick or stone paving patterns. The cuts are then filled with a contrasting render to resemble pointing.

Safety and Environment: Concrete is nontoxic, unless it is used in conjunction with toxic materials such as asbestos, and is made from natural materials, albeit with chemical additives. Sawing concrete generates dust that can be inhaled and causes permanent damage — protective masks must be worn by all in the immediate area.

Availability: Building suppliers and home-improvement retailers stock raw materials and stencils to imprint patterns.

Cost: ❸ Medium.

Specifications: Render is available as powder cement to mix with water and aggregate.

PLASTER &
PLASTER COMPOSITES

Remnants of plaster used as a wall render have been found in Anatolia and Syria, dating back 9,000 years. Gypsum, the principal ingredient of plaster, has featured as an important raw material in the great civilizations of history: the ancient Egyptians used burned and crushed gypsum mixed into cement mortar for constructing the pyramids; the Greeks used gypsum plaster to create smooth wall panels on which to paint frescoes; the Romans used plaster to cast copies of classical Greek marble sculptures. Plaster's versatility allows it to be cast into molds, modeled or carved as a sculptor's material. It has even been used to cast the death masks popular in Victorian times and in forensic investigations for casting imprints.

Gypsum is a sedimentary rock found extensively across northern Europe and North America. There are large deposits around Montmartre, on the edge of Paris, and following London's Great Fire, the King of France ordered intensive mining of local gypsum to make plaster coatings for the wooden houses and buildings of his capital, to inhibit the spread of fire. Montmartre's gypsum gave plaster of Paris its name, which in turn gave its name to Paris, Ontario, where gypsum was widely used in building.

Large quantities of gypsum were imported to England from France during the reign of King Henry VIII, who favored it in the decoration of his lavish new palaces. By this time,

in the 16th century, the technique of applying plaster to walls had evolved from a basic weatherproofing requirement to providing a very smooth surface that could be decorated to a high level with paint and fabrics. The ability to reproduce fine detail in plaster has made it a popular material for many decorative techniques, especially the textured embellishment of walls and ceilings, where it gradually replaced carved wood as a medium for decorative detail.

Where the Tudors favored complex gridwork and stylized flowers, taste in later eras varied from classical Georgian to unrestrained rococo, but ornamental plasterwork on ceilings, crown molding and friezes continued to be a feature, wherever it could be afforded, until the 20th century. Now plaster mostly provides a smooth surface for walls and ceilings that can be kept clean and decorated with paint or paper.

The practice of wet plastering walls is gradually being replaced with prefabricated sheets of plaster, called drywall. These sheets create flat internal surfaces and are easily cut to fit complicated shapes and profiles. Wet plastering is now increasingly seen as a specialist technique for use in restoration projects, or new buildings that seek to maintain the historic use of traditional plaster coatings, which will breathe and move as a building settles.

WOOD • RUBBER, PLASTIC, RESIN & LINOLEUM • METAL • GLASS • FABRIC • PAPER • LEATHER • PAINT, VARNISH & LACQUER • STONE, CERAMICS & TILES • CONCRETE & CEMENT • **PLASTER**

DRYWALL

INTERIOR MATERIALS & SURFACES: THE COMPLETE GUIDE

DRYWALL

Drywall has been widely used since the 1970s as a cheaper alternative to plastering walls. It consists of sheets of hardened plaster sandwiched between two layers of paper, providing a smooth surface onto which to apply a decorative finish. Drywall is quick, easy and clean to apply on site and forms a stable surface for both walls and ceilings.

Properties: Grades of drywall include insulated, acoustic, impact-resistant and moistureproof. Drywall breaks down in damp conditions, so in areas of high moisture use cement board (cement between two layers of mesh) instead. Drywall can aid fireproofing: a layer ½ inch (1.25 cm) thick withstands fire for 30 minutes (two layers 60 minutes). Each side of drywall has a slightly different finish: gray card for wet plaster, white for paint or wallpaper. Drywall requires a skim coat of plaster to disguise the joints unless tapered boards are used, where beveled edges create a groove for filling with joint compound.

Use and Maintenance: Drywall makes a cheaper, easier alternative to wet plaster (or for areas unsuitable for plastering). It is used for ceilings and for partition walls, attached to the studwork instead of wooden laths or EML (expanded metal lath). Attach drywall to lumber supports around the perimeter and at intervals across the surface with drywall screws or nails (adhesive can be used for small pieces). Drywall can be cut with a utility knife: score the top layer of paper, snap the board to break and cut the paper on the other side. Cover joints and fasteners with jointing tape and filler, sanding back when dry, or if a final skim coat is to be applied, cover with tape or gauzelike plasterer's skrim.

Safety and Environment: Airborne plaster dust is hazardous to eyes and when inhaled, so proper safety equipment should be worn. Drywall will biodegrade in wet conditions.

Availability: From building suppliers and home-improvement retailers.

Cost: ❷ Low (high when insulation-backed).

Specifications: Sheets: 4 x 8 ft (1,220 x 2,440 mm), ⅜, ½ or ⅝ in (9, 12.5 or 18 mm) thick. Insulated boards: 1–3 in (25–80 mm) thick.

STRIPPED PLASTER WITH CLAY OR DUNG

Many earth-based products have traditionally been used in and on buildings. Mud or clay mixed with cow dung and straw produces daub, used for wattle-and-daub constructions. Hand-formed into bricks, it is called adobe. Gypsum plaster and cement concrete are modern equivalents, but these natural products are being revived as environmentally friendly alternatives.

Properties: Fresh cow dung mixed with water into a paste can be used as a render in a similar way to plaster. It dries rock hard, is weatherproof and is commonly used in parts of Africa and India. Cow dung was also added to "chinking," the gypsum- or clay-based filling between logs in North American log cabins and houses. Earth, either piled in layers of sod, banked up or dug out, is an effective sound and heat insulator. Historically, buildings were built partially underground and this practice is being revived for environmentally sustainable buildings. Natural plasters and finishes use materials such as clay and sand with straw or similar fibers (for fibrous strength and to reduce shrinkage), and binding agents such as linseed oil, blood, dung or manure, glue or lime, to create breathable, nontoxic and renewable renders. These are not hard-wearing, so must be maintained regularly.

Use and Maintenance: Natural plasters and finishes are enjoying a revival due to the interest in handmade, locally obtainable materials. They are particularly appropriate on new straw bale buildings (see page 233), as they allow the construction to breathe and they fit in with the same ideology. The majority of these traditional materials and techniques are used for the preservation of ancient buildings, but the rise of eco-building and the revival of earth-based products and low-tech production has raised their profile.

Safety and Environment: Care should be taken when handling fresh waste products from any animal. Products are nontoxic when dry and completely environmentally friendly.

Availability: From local farms and fields or clay pits.

Cost: ❷ Low.

Specifications: Wide range of recipes from around the world, dependent on local materials, requirements and weather conditions.

VENETIAN PLASTER

Venetian plaster is a natural material derived from powdered gypsum (calcium sulfate), which is heat treated and mixed with water to form a smooth paste. This can be cast, molded or spread while wet, or modeled and carved once it has dried and solidified. Venetian plaster's main use is for covering walls and ceilings as a ground for a paint or papered decorative finish.

Properties: Venetian plaster has fairly weak hydrogen bonds, so is not exceptionally hard. It cures and hardens without applied heat, expanding slightly while drying, then shrinking again. Once cured, it is stable and will not shrink, so provides a reliably smooth surface. If cured too fast, hairline fractures appear. Ensure plaster is completely dry before sealing, or residual moisture will retreat into the structure. Venetian plaster is usually white, gray or pale pink and has a low surface spread for fire. Specific additives can enhance moisture-proofing or hardness, or promote surface buildup for a textured topcoat.

Use and Maintenance: Venetian plaster can be applied to most solid surfaces, such as brick, stone or concrete, and lumber lath or EML (expanded metal lath). It is also used as a skim coat for drywall (see page 239). On a rough surface, first apply an undercoat, then finish with a smooth topcoat. A finished plaster covering is approximately ⅜ inch (1.5 cm) thick. When dry, seal plaster to avoid discoloration — paint is commonly used, but wax, linseed oil or varnish are alternatives. Venetian plaster can be mixed with pigments, aggregate or fine marble, or glass dust (for a shimmering effect). It can be applied smoothly or with rollers or trowels to provide a textured render. Venetian plaster is reasonably soft, so can be rubbed down with sandpaper after curing.

Safety and Environment: Airborne plaster dust is hazardous to eyes and when inhaled, so proper safety equipment should be worn. Venetian plaster can be broken up and recycled as hardcore.

Availability: From building suppliers and home-improvement retailers.

Cost: ❷ Low.

Specifications: In sacks: 16½, 22 or 55 lbs (7.5, 10 or 25 kg); premixed in containers: 16½ or 22 lbs (7.5 or 10 kg).

WOOD • RUBBER, PLASTIC, RESIN & LINOLEUM • METAL • GLASS • FABRIC • PAPER • LEATHER • PAINT, VARNISH & LACQUER • STONE, CERAMICS & TILES • CONCRETE & CEMENT • PLASTER

CAST PLASTER

INTERIOR MATERIALS & SURFACES: THE COMPLETE GUIDE

CAST PLASTER

Plaster mixed to a very smooth consistency can be cast into simple or complex shapes by using molds. It cures without the application of heat or chemicals, so can be used anywhere to create customized objects. Being a fine material, plaster is excellent for reproducing delicate or intricate textures, such as hand/footprints, feathers, leaves or ornamental carvings, but being fragile, textured low-relief molds are best.

Properties: Casting plaster is a straightforward, fast-setting, general-purpose material used when final hardness is not important. Where durability is important, stone plaster is an extremely hard alternative. As plaster dries and hardens it expands and shrinks, so comes away from a mold smoothly. Neither casting nor stone plasters are waterproof, but a suitable polymer mixed into plaster can make it highly water- and rain-resistant and so suitable for outdoor use. Texture and appearance can be varied by mixing in earth- or water-based pigments, stone fillers, sand, aggregate, marble dust or glass, but a strengthening polymer is advisable with these additives. Unsealed plasters are porous and discolor with airborne grease and dust. Plaster is not flammable.

Use and Maintenance: Plaster casting is a simple process that does not require sophisticated equipment, and articles can be cast as tiles, tabletops, picture frames, decorative surfaces and wallcoverings. Coat items to be cast with a separator such as petroleum jelly. Casting plasters are mixed with water, forming a runny paste suitable for pouring into a mold. The paste should be stirred well and poured slowly, and the molds tamped or agitated to eliminate air bubbles. Cured plasters can be further worked with sandpaper or wire brushes. Plaster is difficult to keep clean, so is best sealed with wax, linseed oil or varnish.

Safety and Environment: Airborne plaster dust is hazardous to eyes and when inhaled, so proper safety equipment should be worn.

Availability: From specialized artist and plaster suppliers, building suppliers and home-improvement retailers.

Cost: ❷ Low.

Specifications: In sacks: 11, 55 or 77 lbs (5, 25 or 35 kg).
Plaster polymer: 2¼, 11 or 55 lbs (1, 5 or 25 kg).

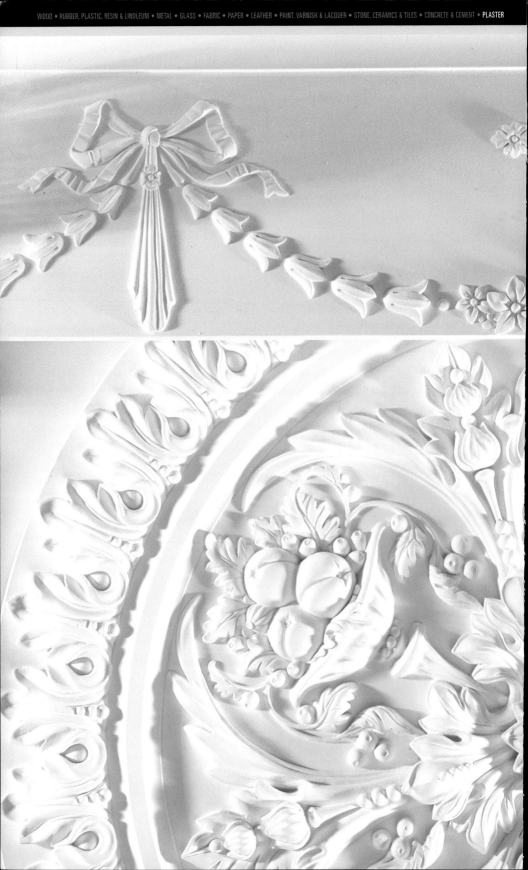

MEDALLIONS AND CROWN MOLDING

Historically, plaster moldings were created in low or high relief, sometimes with ornate pendants hanging from trellised ceilings, and forming decorative geometric or botanical patterns to adorn every internal surface, from ceiling panels and crown molding to illustrative friezes, panels and chair rails. Contemporary use of moldings is usually far more restrained, or gently ironic for a faux historical effect.

Properties: Today architectural features molded in plaster are hand-modeled and cast in fine plaster (to give fine definition to the finished design), usually with a primed finish ready for painting. Plaster is not particularly hard and can be damaged by impact. It is not flammable. Unsealed plasters are porous and discolor with airborne grease and dust. Increasingly, imitation plaster moldings are being produced in polyurethane. There are a limited number of moldings available for ceiling and wall panels: niches, cartouches, ceiling medallions, friezes, pilasters (half columns), door and fireplace surrounds, chair rails and faux structural brackets. Cornicing is one of the few products still widely used in a variety of styles.

Use and Maintenance: Plaster moldings are used both for restoration work and new installations. Architectural moldings are usually based on historical European Georgian, Victorian and Edwardian styles. Crown moldings are the most commonly available in any variety, from simple quarter-round styles to architectural patterns such as rectangular dentillation, classic egg-and-dart and acanthus leaf designs. New lengths of plaster molding can be manufactured to match original lengths for infill sections or for new rooms. The details in original moldings become blurred as they are filled in with successive layers of paint, so, although expensive, it is worth having paint periodically stripped out when redecorating moldings.

Safety and Environment: Airborne plaster dust is hazardous to eyes and when inhaled, so proper safety equipment should be worn. Plaster can be broken up and recycled as hardcore.

Availability: From specialized plaster moldings suppliers, interior-design stores, building suppliers and home-improvement retailers.

Cost: ❹ High.

Specifications: Ceiling medallions in about 8 patterns: 14–42 in (350–1,075 mm) diameter. Crown moldings in about 8 styles: usually 2½ or 3¾ in (65 or 96 mm) deep in 8 ft (2,440 mm) lengths.

USEFUL CONTACTS

WOOD

Wood Flooring International
Phone: 856-764-2501
E-mail: wfi@wflooring.com
www.wflooring.com

Pergo
Phone: 1-800-33-PERGO/1-800-337-3746
www.pergo.com/Pergo/US_Home
Laminate flooring

Sylvan Brandt
Phone: 717-626-4520
E-mail: dean@sylvanbrandt.com
www.sylvanbrandt.com
Antique wood flooring and salvaged building materials

Carlisle Wide Plank Floors
Phone: 1-800-595-9663
E-mail: info@wideplankflooring.com
www.wideplankflooring.com
New and antique wide plank flooring

Natural Cork Inc.
Phone: 1-800-404-2675
www.naturalcork.com

RUBBER, PLASTIC, RESIN & LINOLEUM

Polymeric Systems Inc.
Phone: 1-800-228-5548
E-mail: info@polymericsystems.com
www.polymericsystems.com
Epoxies for wood and masonry restoration and metal repair

R.C.A. Rubber
Phone: 330-784-1291 or 1-800-321-2340
E-mail: info@rcarubber.com
www.rcarubber.com
Sheet rubber flooring

Armstrong Floors
Phone: 1-800-233-3823
www.armstrong.com/resna/res_floors.jsp
Vinyl and linoleum flooring (also hardwood and ceramics)

METAL

Hygrade Polishing and Plating Co.
Phone: 718-392-4082
E-mail: info@hygradeplating.com
www.hygradeplating.com
Metal plating and refinishing

W. H. Coe Inc.
Phone: 860-524-8811
E-mail: whcoe@snet.net
www.whcoe.com
Gold leaf and gilding supplies

Sepp Leaf Products Inc.
Phone: 212-683-2840
E-mail: sales@seppleaf.com
www.seppleaf.com
Gold leaf and other decorative finish materials

Foundry Art Fine Bronze
Phone: 773-784-2628
E-mail: foundryart@lowitzandcompany.com
www.lowitzandcompany.com/foundryart

Steptoe & Wife Antiques Ltd.
Phone: 1-800-461-0060 or 416-780-1707
E-mail: info@steptoewife.com
www.steptoewife.com
Victorian cast-iron staircases and metalwork

GLASS

Bendheim
Phone: 212-226-6370
www.bendheim.com
Importers and distributors of specialty glass

Glass Block U.S.A.
www.glassblockusa.com
A family of glass block companies serving residential,
commercial and industrial applications

FABRIC

Beacon Fabric & Notions
Phone: 1-800-713-8157 or 727-347-5663
E-mail: sales@beaconfabric.com
www.beaconfabric.com

Fabrics-Store.com
Phone: 1-888-LINEN54 (546-3654) or 323-465-8050
www.fabrics-store.com

Fabulous-Furs
Phone: 1-800-848-4650
www.fabulousfurs.com
Faux fur

Carpet One
www.carpetone.com
Wide range of carpets; also vinyl, hardwood and laminates

Unique Carpets Ltd.
Phone: 909-352-8125
E-mail: info@uniquecarpetsltd.com
www.uniquecarpetsltd.com

PAPER
Brewster Wallcovering Company
Phone: 1-800-366-1700
www.brewsterwallcovering.com
Wallcoverings and fabrics

Blonder Wallcoverings
Phone: 1-800-321-4070
E-mail: Blonderwall@blonderhome.com
www.blonderwall.com

Bradbury & Bradbury Art Wallpapers
Phone: 707-746-1900
E-mail: info@bradbury.com
www.bradbury.com
Victorian new classical and Arts & Crafts wallpapers

Twinrocker Handmade Paper
Phone: 1-800-757-TWIN (8946) or 765-563-3119
E-mail: twinrocker@twinrocker.com
www.twinrocker.com

LEATHER
Edelman Leather
Phone: 860-350-9600 or 1-800-886-TEDY
www.edelmanleather.com

PAINT, VARNISH & LACQUER
Benjamin Moore Paints
US
E-mail: info@benjaminmoore.com
www.benjaminmoore.com
Canada
Phone: 1-800-361-5898
www.benjaminmoore.ca
House paints and industrial coatings

The Old Fashioned Milk Paint Co.
Phone: 978-448-6336
E-mail: anne@milkpaint.com
www.milkpaint.com
Chemically safe historic paints in 16 colors

Old Village Paints
Phone: 1-800-498-7687
E-mail: info@old-village.com
www.old-village.com

STONE, CERAMICS & TILES
Bedrosians
E-mail: bedrosians@aol.com
www.bedrosians.com

Dakota Granite
Phone: 1-800-843-3333
www.dakgran.com
Granite tile and custom granite products

Century Tile
www.century-tile.com
Wide range of tiles; also vinyl, hardwood, carpet and laminates

Talisman Handmade Tiles
Phone: 773-784-2628
E-mail: talisman@lowitzandcompany.com
www.lowitzandcompany.com/talisman

Terrapin Tile
Phone: 989-821-3320
E-mail: leslie@terrapintile.com
www.terrapintile.com

Limestone Concept Inc.
Phone: 310-278-9829
E-mail: stoneconcept@earthlink.net
www.limestoneconcept.com
Imported limestone and terra-cotta

CONCRETE & CEMENT
Stepstone Inc.
Phone: 1-800-572-9029
www.stepstoneinc.com
Precast concrete products

Tile Tech
Phone: 323-733-6187
E-mail: sales@paversetc.com
www.tiletechusa.com
Specialists in precast European concrete pavers

PLASTER
Fischer & Jirouch Co.
Phone: 216-361-3840
www.fischerandjirouch.com
Hand-crafted plaster moldings

Felber Ornamental Plastering Corp.
Phone: 1-800-392-6896 or 610-275-4713
E-mail: jk@felber.net
www.felber.net
Manufacturers of ornamental plaster

GLOSSARY

a

acanthus conventionalized leaf pattern based on a Mediterranean plant, used to decorate plaster moldings in the style of the capitals of Egyptian and Corinthian columns.

acid-bitten the corrosive effect on the surface of glass when exposed to hydrofluoric acid.

acoustic underlay a rigid or flexible material laid beneath floorcovering made of material to absorb the transmission of airborne or impact sound.

adobe unbaked brick dried by the sun used for house building.

aggregate a dense, chemically inert material, usually gravel or sand, providing the bulk in concrete.

alloy a mixture of metals to transform the properties of one metal.

anaglypta wallpaper embossed with a raised pattern of flowers, leaves or geometric or random shapes.

analine dye synthetic dye not dependent on natural pigment.

annealed heated to red hot and cooled very slowly to control surface strength.

architectural glass custom-made decorative glass items designed for particular installations.

archival paper acid-free paper used for picture mats or for protection and storage of fine art or photographs.

b

baluster the turned post of a balustrade.

balustrade a series of balusters supporting a handrail.

barrel vault (or tunnel vault) where the ceiling is semicircular in shape, like a half-barrel lying on its side.

baseboard flat board, often with a molded top portion, used as a trim at the base of a wall.

bas relief raised sculptural pattern, such as seen on the pediment of the Parthenon and other classical buildings.

borax an alkali chemical to aid bonding of milk-based paints and glues. It is poisonous and often mixed with sugar to kill rats.

broadloom carpet produced on a loom wider than 6 ft (1.8 m), generally in rolls 13–16 ft (4–5 m) wide to cover entire floors of rooms as "wall-to-wall" carpet.

buff to polish the surface of a material to a shiny finish. In bricks, a yellowish beige color of clay.

bullnose half-round shaped profile to the front edge of a shelf or trim.

c

calcium caseinate a curdlike extract from skim milk used to make milk paints.

capital the decorative top portion of a column or pilaster.

carcassing internal sides, top and base of closets or cabinets intended to be covered with additional finishing material.

carreaux d'octagone pattern of floor tiling where the corners are removed from square tiles to form irregular octagons and small contrasting square tiles are laid at their intersection.

cartouche heavily molded round or oval detail placed on walls high over doors or in corners, originally to exhibit coats of arms.

cement board a variety of boards produced of cement, often up to 50 percent recycled, manufactured to replace products that would otherwise be made of wood. Special qualities, such as acoustic, weather- or rodent-resistant or vandalproof boards, are produced for particular applications.

certification confirmation that material is legitimately acquired from a sustainable source.

chair rail a horizontal molding on the wall of a room, originally used to protect against damage caused by chairbacks.

chamfer a small 45-degree angle shaved off the edge of wood boards to take away the sharp edge and create a finished look.

chinking the gypsum- or clay-based material used to fill the gaps between lumber in log cabins in the U.S. and Canada.

clapboard *see* weatherboarding.

clear float glass very regular, flat and clear glass formed by floating molten glass on a bath of molten tin.

composite containing a mixture of materials.

compound a substance consisting of two or more elements chemically combined.

coping a sloped capping or covering to protect the top of a wall from weather damage.

Corinthian a building style of classical Greek and Roman architecture characterized by the acanthus leaf pattern.

coving plain crown molding with a quarter-round concave profile.

cracked irregular pattern resembling the random effect of crackle glaze.

craquelure the distinctive pattern of hairline cracking found on old master paintings.

crown molding decorative horizontal molding at the junction of ceiling and wall.

crystalline having a structure of crystals.

cuerda seca designs that imitate the complex geometric or floral patterns of the Moorish and Spanish traditional tiling.

cure setting of liquid material to a hard finish.

d
deckled an irregular torn or frayed edge on handmade paper.

dentilled crown molding pattern of regular, rectangular, tooth-like projections based on the classical Greek Ionic order, and imitating an architectural feature where the roof structure is visible below the eaves.

die an engraved stamp for impressing or perforating a design on sheet material.

distemper water-based paint.

dormer projection set into the side of a roof usually containing a window.

drywall practice of using prefabricated dried sheets of plaster, or plasterboard, to provide a smooth wall surface, replacing the traditional technique of wet plastering.

e
eaves the part of a sloping roof that overhangs a wall.

efflorescence powdery white salt deposit on the face of bricks created by the movement of water through brickwork.

egg-and-dart crown molding pattern where an egg shape is repeated along the crown molding with a sharp arrowhead projecting down between each egg.

eggshell low sheen of paint or varnish finish between matte and gloss.

elastic bending movement the point at which metal will spring back when bent, before the point at which it will retain the new shape.

EML (expanded metal lath) sheet metal cut in a grid of tiny slashed cuts and pulled to open a curve in each cut. Used stretched over studwork, it makes a rough surface onto which to apply wet plaster.

encaustic paint hot wax-based paints developed in ancient Greece and today made with beeswax, pigment and resin.

encaustic tiles low-gloss earthenware tiles with complex geometric inlaid patterns of colored clay.

f
fanlight a window above a door, often semicircular with a radiating fan pattern of glazing bars.

ferrous containing iron.

film thin sheet of clear plastic or oil, used alone, as a surface finish.

flashed on tiles, a burn mark that produces a colored effect, which graduates from black to brown across the surface.

flutes vertical channels cut into the shaft of a column or pilaster.

frieze decorative area of wall between the crown molding and the picture rail.

furrings strips of lumber on which to hang a finishing material.

g
galvanized noncorrosive finish applied by immersing in molten zinc.

gilding the process of coating an object in gold leaf.

glass slags a nonmetallic silica- (sand) based product formed in the firing process, which can help control the firing.

grosgrain woven ribbon with an even texture of lateral ridges.

ground a base or substrate for application of a decorative finish.

gypsum calcium sulfate found in large natural deposits in the ground, used in the manufacture of plaster.

h

hardcore coarse rubble used to provide a stable base below concrete foundations or paving.

hydrophilic attracting and absorbing water readily.

i

igneous rock that has solidified from volcano lava or magma deep in the Earth's crust.

in register two patterns, perhaps one printed and one embossed, that are aligned.

j

jacquard fabric where the weave is more dense in some areas, or the fibers are shinier, to make an organic or paisley pattern without change of color.

japanned painted and varnished in imitation of oriental lacquerwork. Also a matte black enamel finish on ironwork.

joinery finished woodwork used for doors, windows, stairs, etc.

joists horizontal lumber laid parallel to form the structure of a floor or ceiling.

l

laid fine horizontally ridged texture of paper.

lath thin horizontal strips of rough lumber providing a tooth onto which to apply plaster, wooden lath has largely been replaced by expanded metal lath (EML).

leaded lights small panes of glass connected with lead strips to form windows.

m

machined profile run through a machine like a router or spindle molder with a shaped blade to form a particular outline, such as the projecting "tongue" and inset "groove" of tongue and groove boards.

marbleized painted or stained to resemble marble.

marquetry picture or pattern formed from small pieces of inlaid colored veneers as seen on backgammon boards or closet doors.

medallion radiating molded plaster ceiling feature, often with a pendant light suspended in its center.

moiré fabric or wallpaper that has been treated to have a watered or wavelike appearance, but with no change of color.

mullion wooden dividing post in a window.

mylar clear or silver film used for wrapping flowers (clear) and for helium balloons or packages of cookies (silver).

n

nap raised pile on textiles such as velvet and fur.

niche hollowed-out area with a decorative surround to contain a small ornament or light.

nosing applied or solid strip of lumber at the exposed edge of a sheet, shelf or stair tread either to give a hard-wearing or smooth decorative edge.

p

parapet a low wall surrounding the roof of a building.

pavers concrete or natural stone slabs cut or cast to regular sizes for use as paving.

pediment the triangular termination of a roof bounded by horizontal and sloping crown moldings in classical architecture; may be plain or decorated in bas relief sculpture.

perma-press fabrics manufactured with a polyester component to retain a smooth pressed appearance even after machine washing.

petrochemical a chemical substance derived from petroleum.

picture rail horizontal molding to the upper portion of a wall from which pictures are hung.

pilasters half columns attached flat against a wall.

pile arrangement of threads standing upright, as in carpets or velvet.

pilling small balls of loose fibers of the material that collect on the surface of knitted cloth.

plate metal material applied to the surface of an object.

pointing cement mortar bonding brick or block.

postformed prefabricated backsplash and bullnose.

prelaminated glued together under heat and pressure under factory conditions.

pressure-treated a preservative treatment for lumber, which can increase water resistance, often leaving a visible greenish tinge.

primer a surface treatment used to prepare a bond for a finishing treatment.

r

render to texture; cement render: a surface coat of cement applied for a smooth or textured/stamped finish.

reveal inner surface of a door or window opening.

riven a texture typical of stone that has been split (resembling the surface of a slate tile), with smooth diagonal ridges.

routered carved with a machine.

ruched loosely pleated, fluted or crimped fabric.

rusticated Renaissance style of heavily textured masonry with exaggerated deep joints used as an external surface finish to the lower stories of buildings.

s

seasoned dried to the required extent for intended use.

selvage densely woven finished edging of a length of cloth to prevent unraveling or distortion.

sheer a very thin, sometimes translucent fabric or material.

sheering surface tension.

shingle tiles of wood or asphalt used for roofing or exterior wallcoverings.

shute the weft fibers of a metal cloth or mesh.

sill horizontal board at the base of a window frame.

size a natural glue product that gives a shiny, stiff finish to paper or cloth.

skiving edge-finishing technique for leather that does not increase thickness.

skrim loosely woven cotton net fabric used to strengthen cast plaster.

slubbed yarn spun with bunches of untwisted fibers at intervals which, when woven, provide an occasional horizontal thickness, as seen in linen and dupion silk.

soffit underside of beam, arch, stairs, window or door opening.

steel rebar steel reinforcing bar set into concrete to increase the strength in tension of the concrete.

stock rags or paper from which paper is made.

stove enamel polyester powder coating, baked-on factory finish for metal fixtures.

studwork partitions made of upright lumber with drywall on each side to make an internal wall.

substrate the utilitarian surface to which a decorative or durable surface is applied.

surface fire spread the extent to which a material encourages or contributes to the spread of fire.

t

tessellated complex geometric floor patterns based on the marble mosaic floors of Italian churches.

tongue and groove profiled lumber boards where one side is grooved and the other has a projecting tongue fitting into the groove to provide a joint.

tooth texture of surface that will promote adhesion of paint, plaster or dye.

trim a vertical return at the perimeter of a linoleum or terrazzo floor finish or along the rear edge of the worktop to form an unbroken joint with the horizontal surface.

truss triangulated structural support for roofs or bridges.

v

vinyl siding thermoplastic external cladding for walls that looks like wooden shiplap or weatherboarding.

vitreous enamel a finish formed by heating and melting powdered glass and pigment to a material like metal or glass.

w

wainscot the lower portion of a wall between the chair rail and baseboard, often paneled or covered with decorative wallpaper.

warp the threads arranged on a loom that extend lengthwise along a bolt of fabric. *See also* weft.

weatherboarding overlapping boards providing an external cladding over lumber framework. Also known as clapboard and shiplap.

weft the threads carried on a shuttle back and forth across the warp threads from selvage to selvage.

INDEX

ACKNOWLEDGMENTS

The publisher would like to thank the following for their assistance and for the loan of materials:

African Treasures, Harrow

Atlantic Rubber Ltd., Altrincham

Auro Organic Paints, Saffron Walden

Barron Glass, Cheltenham

Teresa Bell, Selby

Berwyn Slate Quarry Ltd., Llangollen

Bridgwater Filters Ltd., West Bromwich

R. K. Burt & Company Ltd., London

Chameleon Collection, Alcester

Kenneth Clark Ceramics Ltd., Lewes

Divine Art & Craft Ltd., Horsham

Edelman Leather, New Milford

English Hurdle Somerset, Taunton

Fabulous-Furs, Covington

Flecotex, Alicante

Forbo-Nairn Ltd., Kirkcaldy

Foundry Art Fine Bronze, Chicago

International, St Ives

Ipswich Plastics Ltd., Ipswich

Lochcarron of Scotland, Galashiels

Luxcrete Ltd., London

Med Imports, Augusta

MLC Ltd, Lincoln

Natural Cork Inc., Augusta

Old Village Paints Ltd., Fort Washington

Plastic Extruders Ltd, Wickford

Puddle Lodge Crafts, Aberdeen

The Real Sheepskin Association, Northampton

Ruabon, Wrexham

Simply Stained (David Lilly) Brighton, *www.simply-stained.*

Smith Brothers Ltd., Portsmouth

SPA Laminates Ltd., Leeds

Stevensons of Norwich, Norwich

Talisman Handmade Tiles, Chicago

Terrapin Tile, Roscommon

Jo Vincent Glass Design, Kendal

Welsh Slate, Bangor

Wessex Resins & Adhesives Limited, Romsey

Wookey Hole Papermill, Wookey Hole

The York Handmade Brick Co. Ltd., York

Helen Bowers would like to thank the following people for their help:
Henry Bowers, Jennifer Bowers, Caroline Ball, Gerry Judah, Julius Judah, Raphael Judah, Natasha Lomas, Ilana Pearlman, Nicki Schmiegelow, Peggy Vance, Brenda Webster, Judy Wiseman